NAM:
OUR
LEGACY

DAN RAPP

Acknowledgements

This book would never have started without the encouragement of Greta Baker Allen. Her brother Curt's story is told in Chapter 2. My thanks to long time friend George Navadel who really got me started with something tangible. His DVD *An Infantry Company's Tale* provided details otherwise not obtainable.

Recollections from Rev. Joe O'Donnell CSC, Paul Reinman, Charlie Jager, Tofie Owen, Corwin Kippenhan, Jack Conlon, Bob Hall, Dennis O'Hare and George Navadel brought to the text personal experiences of the war in Vietnam and the homecoming.

I did not serve in Vietnam. I left the Air Force in 1963, but I admire the men and women who did serve there. It was, after all, a noble cause for liberty and freedom for a people unable to defend them selves.

The stories are about people I know, knew or were somehow connected through the media or my alma mater Notre Dame. Bless them all, save two.

NAM: OUR LEGACY

DELIVER US FROM EVIL

I had seen Dr. Tom Dooley speak at the Notre Dame Navy Drill Hall in 1959. He was eloquent, organized, a natural, gifted speaker. At the time he was touted as one of us although he never got an under graduate degree from Notre Dame. He had moved on to St. Louis University and then to medical school there. All of that was immaterial when he gave his presentation about Southeast Asia.

Dooley listed a litany of atrocities perpetrated by the Communists in Southeast Asia and followed with a litany of refugee benefactors from America's pharmacy industry. After the fall of Dien Bien Phu the demarcation between North and South Vietnam receded southward until the borders were stabilized with a demilitarized zone (DMZ) between the two. Ninety-five thousand refugees fled south, five thousand fled north. It was here that he first saw the atrocities as a Navy doctor.

Tom Dooley traversed the states giving speeches and soliciting funds for refugee relief. With the purpose of continuing his humanitarian work he left the Navy. Politically he was against the Communists and *for* whoever opposed them. He had seen the atrocities first hand and didn't hesitate talking about them in great detail. His humanitarian work consumed his physical and his mental energies and despite declining health he returned to Laos.

By then he was the image of the righteous American in a justified crusade against evil. In 1956 he had published a book entitled "Deliver Us from Evil," a best seller. The book and the road tour of speeches put Tom in the middle of the political tension that never ceased after Vietnam was split into two countries. He was the advocate of democracy and freedom moreso than the President of South Vietnam, Ngo Dinh Diem.

When Ho Chi Minh began supporting the insurgent Viet Cong the government in the south pleaded for aid from the U.S. Arms and advisers began to flow into South Viet Nam....slowly.

By 1960 Dr. Tom was awarded an honorary doctorate by Notre Dame. To the anti-communist coalition he was the poster boy, the rallying figure who could sway public opinion to sympathize with South Vietnam. He was the first face of America in the troubled Southeast Asia that was about to boil over.

Dr. Tom Dooley (1927-1961)

The Gulf of Tonkin

August 2, 1964

Two American destroyers came under attack from North Vietnamese torpedo boats while assisting South Vietnamese naval forces. Quickly, USS Maddox and USS C. Turner Joy reported to the fleet headquarters.

Two days later more attacks were reported, but then the plot thickens. While nervous sonar operators on the destroyers caused radar controlled guns to fire, aircraft from carriers Ticonderoga and Constellation launched towards an unseen enemy.

Squadron Commander James Stockdale (later a POW in the Hanoi Hilton) reported no sight of North Vietnamese torpedo boats. From his perch above the sea he saw only American ships and fired his guns at imaginary torpedoes in the water amid radio messages screaming, "Torpedoes in the water. Torpedoes in the water."

Was it faulty interpretation by National Security Agency of North Vietnamese radio transmissions or simply inexperienced naval personnel that caused the fracas? Years later nobody could answer.

In 1995 Vo Nguyen Giap supreme commander of all North Vietnamese forces told Robert McNamara (former Secretary of Defense) that his torpedo boats chased an American destroyer from his territorial waters on August 2nd, but denied any action on the 4th.

The after action reports went to Washington on August 5th and the Gulf of Tonkin Resolution (HJ RES 1145) was born. Shortly thereafter Navy airpower struck the North Vietnamese torpedo boat maintenance docks and fuel facilities at Hon Me and Hon Ngu.

In 2005 NSA historian Robert J. Hanyok disclosed that NSA had deliberately skewed intelligence reports to cover up a series of previous intelligence mistakes but it was not a politically motivated ploy.

The Resolution gave Presidents Johnson and Nixon the power for escalating the involvement in the Indochina struggle with world Communism. America would pay with 58,000 lives and 150 billions of dollars. And Communism (The National Liberation Front) would win and curse Southeast Asia for two decades.

After 1975 the Vietnamese Army would grow not shrink and go to war with both China and Cambodia. The American political left didn't seem to mind the hundreds of thousands killed after we left. After all they were all Asians and all Communists.

Internal strife left two million dead in Cambodia at the hands of Pol Pot and the Khmer Rouge. Another half million died In Laos, victims of the Pathet Lao. The political left continued to deny the Domino theory but the mountain of skulls rose higher in the Killing Fields.

ONE

CONTACT IMMINENT

For those who man the battle line
The bugle whispers low.
For freedom has a taste and price
The protected never know.

May 31, 2010

Only the altar lights kept the church from being in total darkness. The parishioners were sparsely dispersed throughout the pews of St. Thomas Moore Catholic Church in Oceanside, California. It was Memorial Day and 0750 hours.

One parishioner stood out among the few as he walked the center aisle to the fifth row. Dressed in his dress blues, he carried a white garrison cap cradled in his left arm. A mirror finish shined from his black shoes and silver eagles adorned his shoulder epaulets.

Thirty years a Marine, everybody knew who he was and why he was there at mass. Col. George D. Navadel – USMC Retired was fulfilling his annual ritual of remembrance. Seven men had died in his command and as long as he lived they would never be forgotten. The Wall in Washington carried their names but they were also etched in his heart and in his mind, especially on Memorial Day.

He genuflected and entered the pew, signing himself with the sign of the cross as he did. As he knelt the faces of the seven filed passed in review, men he had only briefly known, six Marines and one Navy medical corpsman.

His memory bank began unloading the parts he couldn't or wouldn't forget. The words of the new battalion commanding officer (CO) echoed in his head, "Contact imminent." He could relate to the Marines going into Tarawa or Iwo, "Contact imminent."

Broken jungle plants, wheel tracks from heavy machine guns, a mutilated snake, signs enough to know the CO was correct. A last minute warning to a new medical corpsman, "You are not to do a damn thing unless your squad leader tells you," resounded in his memory.

Trudging through the brush in a thickly wooded area makes for heavy breathing. He could hear his own breathing and maybe his heart beat- or was it? He wasn't sure. Three hours of marching were interrupted by the unmistakable rattle of AK-47 and machine gun fire. Lima Company, the other unit on his right flank, had found the enemy.

George had lost six Marines in previous engagements and his priority was to accomplish the mission and minimize casualties. *How do you do that?* He asked himself. The other statistic was also there- ninety-six confirmed NVA (North Vietnam Army). Ahead lay Hill 94, the opportunity to add to the enemy total. *Cruel, Heartless, playing a meaningless game of statistics? Not here. Not in Viet Nam. The politics of the war were already in play with five years to go. Enemy body counts, our own casualties, everything mattered and nothing mattered. It was Nam.*

With Lima Company in the grips of a horseshoe ambush, the plea for help came quickly over the battalion tactical (TAC)

16

radio. The response of Mike Company was immediate, bursting through the cover of the woods they caught the enemy aiming in the opposite direction. Five NVA fell in an instant, Alstott and Pena wounded. Navadel exhorted his Marines, "Sight alignment and trigger squeeze. Hold 'em and sqeeze 'em." A hail of fire broke through the bamboo stalks overhead, splinters everywhere. Sergeants Johnson and Hamm fell wounded.

The M-60 machine guns tore up each succeeding NVA position as Marines hurled grenades and rushed through the resulting smoke. As George attempted to throw a white phosphorous grenade, a tree limb reached out and grabbed his arm, causing the grenade to fall short. A small depression in the earth shaped the explosion, sparing him injury. Overhead, the battalion CO's helicopter poured fire into the panicky NVA as they retreated down the hillside. Oddly, his reference marker turned out to be the smoke from the errant grenade

Navadel was on the verge of giddy, things were going so well, and then the damper, "We have a KIA, Skipper."

"Killed in Action," it's a phrase that jumps out at you, like saying "cancer" when you're talking about a loved one. "Who is it?" he asked. Swallowing hard, he weathered the reply, "The new corpsman, Larry Knight."

Corpsman Larry Knight had done what he was told not to do; he went to the aid of a wounded Marine ahead of the squad. He'd only been in country two days. *How could he know? How could he restrain himself with a Marine writhing in agony and spouting blood? Larry Knight, God, I am sorry. God, I'm sorry for your family.* Navadel turned away preferring to hide his grief, wiping his nose, clearing his eyes, trying vainly to rid himself of the constriction in his throat.

A moment later he was shaken from his dreams, or were they prayers? A priest stood at the side of the altar, "Let us begin with the sign of the cross- In the name of the Father and of the Son and of the Holy Spirit."

The responses rolled off his tongue, but his mind was full of

17

thirty second one act plays. Hectic, stressful, second guessing himself at every other thought. Bullets whizzed by, mortars went *Whump,* men falling, blood soaking their clothing and corpsman rushing to their aid seemingly unaware of the danger.

"Christ has died, Christ is risen, Christ will come again." Back to the mass, the transitions continue to and fro until Communion. ."Lord, I am not worthy to receive you, only say the word and I shall be healed."

Returning to his seat he said a short prayer of thanksgiving and unfolded a piece of paper, "I pray that these seven men are in a place of light and peace, in the presence of our Lord Jesus Christ: Corpsman Larry Knight, SSgt. Guy M. Hodgkins, Cpl. Lorenza Gayles, LCpl. Patrick J. Hannon, LCpl John F. O'Connor, Pvt. David C. DeWitt."

The priest made the sign of the cross over the congregation, "Go in peace to love and serve the Lord." George walked slowly down the aisle to the exit, smiling at fellow parishioners. A few waved politely. Placing his cap on his head he realized, *Tomorrow is June first, the anniversary of the battle on Hill 94, Operation Cimarron. Gosh, forty-three years. I wonder what Machine Gunner Thomlason is doing. Maybe he'll be at the reunion in September.*

CONTACT IMMINENT

Corpsman
(Dedicated to Doc Larry Knight)

Corpsman! Corpsman! A muffled cry echoed through the dark.
High above a Very pistol illuminates the night.
Eerie figures back and forth but no one did I see.
The voice was clear enough, just over to the right.
At last the flare had fallen and darkness fell with it.
Again I heard his feeble voice, can't wait 'til morning's light.

In the darkness slowly, I found the stricken man
Applied a clamp, some sulfa drug, pin closed the nasty cut.
It doesn't sound like much unless that man was you
And a guy with a cross of red was there to save your butt.
Tho in the service there's something else I'd really rather be
I don't know what it is exactly, I just can't say what.

Dogface infantry, artillery, quartermaster corps?
Naw! On second thought, I'm a corpsman through and through.
I guess I really knew it when I saved that very first.
Taking care of guys in need, it's what I ought to do.
Something deep inside decided long ago,
So I wear the cross of red and pledge my life to you.

Col. George D. Navadel USMC
Notre Dame 1958

TWO

MY BROTHER

Dong Ha, 1967:

Lt. Curtis Barker USN spoke into the microphone above the *pffftt, pffftt, pffftt* of the rotor blades and the whine of the turbo jet engine. "Jack, I love this Huey. I love flying. Being a doctor is my vocation but flying is right behind it."

Maj. Jack Owens, USMC smiled, glancing to his right, "You'd make a good helo pilot, Curt, but a lot of good helo pilots wouldn't make good doctors. At least you've got your priorities straight."

Below they could see the Marine fire base, smoke drifting from several fires floated to the north east in one stratified cloud. A tornado of beige dust swirled around their Huey as they touched down. Grim faced Marines, some bare to the waist, pushed the wounded aboard. Four canvas and aluminum stretchers slid across the floor of the helo.

"Three wounded, one KIA," yelled a Navy corpsman. Curt was already examining one man with a head wound. He appeared the worst of the three. Curt knew that large splatters of blood didn't always reveal the worst, most life-threatening problem. In that regard, the other two did look bad. One man spoke freely, propping his head on his elbow. "Doc, Y'all take care o'them fust. I'll be okay." His pant legs were torn open nearly to the crotch. Curt could see where a corpsman had put a series of safety pins to hold closed the holes from the mortar frags.

The second man was unconscious but breathing, he checked his heart beat. The breathing was labored, a bullet through the lung and an ugly exit wound; a gurgling sound accompanied each breath. Tiny red splatters covered his face.

The head wound patient stirred for a moment, his eyes opening wide. An IV bottle swayed at the roof, the tubing leading to his arm. "What the hell's going on?" he said.

"You've been hit, Marine. We're med-evacing you for treatment." Curt answered.

"No, no, that won't do, Doc. You gotta get me back to my unit. I'm the platoon sergeant. They won't know what to do. They're mostly green-horns."

Slowly, he forced a plastic tube down the throat of the patient with the lung shot. His breathing eased, the gurgling stopped. When he turned back to the leg wound patient the man was unconscious. Blood poured from an unseen abdomen wound. Curt frantically unbuttoned the man's jacket, placing a clamp on the blood vessel. A plasma IV joined the other and swayed with every movement of the helo. He checked his eyes, lifting each lid and then placed a stethoscope to his chest, counting each pulse beat.

With the metal floor slippery with blood, Curt moved flat footed between the three, checking vital signs. It seemed like it was taking forever to get to Da Nang. Jack Owens talked hurriedly on the radio, warning the people on the ground what to expect.

A nervous gunner tried to watch the terrain below, but couldn't help but watch the medical professional controlling the situation. *Back home, he'd never see three patients that bad at one time. If he did he'd have a staff of people to help. Here he just has himself. Damn, he's good.*

Finally the chopper set on the pad outside the hospital. A half dozen nurses and corpsmen rushed to take the patients away, Curt trailing behind with the prognoses.

Suddenly, he realized the fourth man was still in the chopper. Turning slowly, he walked back to the open door. The form in the plastic body bag lay still. Curt pulled on the zipper, opening the bag, peering in.

The face was white with death. His hair matted with his own dried blood. *Was he eighteen yet? He didn't look it.* Curt checked his pulse- *nothing.* The wound was massive, left side chest. *Something big had hit this young Marine. He was dead before he hit the ground.* Curt thought a moment and realized he had presumed him dead simply because he was in a body bag. *I'll never do that again, never. I'll never fail to at least give them a chance to survive. That's my job. Dammit.*

He closed the bag. Only then was he aware of the two corpsmen waiting at the door. "Should we take him now, Doc?" One of them asked.

Curt nodded. He couldn't speak. In his hand he held a bloody dog tag. With his sleeve he cleaned it enough to read. Repeating the name twice, he handed it to the corpsman. *A boy, they've sent a boy to fight this awful war. He could have been my kid brother.*

OOO

26 March, 1972
Dear Mom & Dad,

Today is Easter Sunday and out here it is just another day. I hope you received the orchid from Hawaii.

As you may know by now there has been an increase in activity on the part of the enemy during the past month especially in the I Corps area (from Chu Lai north to the DMZ). This has not greatly affected the Medical Dept here at Mag-16 but it has been hard on our aircraft and crews. The Med Evacs have increased greatly and my corpsmen are doing a great job.

One of these days my CO is going to get General Robert Shaw to present me my two Air Medals and my Navy Commendation Medal. Along with this the Marine Corps likes to send out hometown news releases. So if you don't mind, please send me the name of the local newspaper at Paragould and you'll have a hero on your hands when I get back.

The weather is finally clearing up so everyone is feeling better. The temps are now in the 80's in the day and low 70's at night. The rains finally quit so everyone is taking out their clothes and drying them out.

I have slightly less than 31/2 months left in-country and I am looking forward to returning home. This has been a long tour but I'm getting tired of this mess. As of yet I have no word of what my next duty station will be. I should hear definitely by May.

When I returned from Hawaii I spent a few days (10) here and then went to Dong Ha for a week. However we are short of personnel right now so I'll have to go back to Dong ha on the 28th until April 2nd.

Things have been busy here at the dispensary for me. It has not been the sick call or physical exams but the paper work. I am next in line for senior Medical Officer and consequently I am doing much of the paper work. One thing about the military is that everyone loves reports and there is a report to be made on everything. Sometimes I feel someone is sitting over at Wing Medical and thinking of things for us to write reports about.

Well, it is near 6PM and time for Evening Mass.

Love Always,
Curt

OOO

MY BROTHER

28 March, 1967

Jack Owens was doing his preflight check when Curtis approached the Huey. The sun dipped in the west, balancing on the horizon. "Ready to log in thirty minutes, Curt?" he asked.

"I just happen to have my gear with me. What's the mission?" answered Curt.

"We have reports of NVA activity in the area. We're just gonna cruise the perimeter to see if they're here yet. Hop in and strap yourself down. I'm almost done with preflight."

Curt strapped himself in, connecting his radio/intercom cable. Crew chief Cpl Paul Albano and gunner Pfc George Stevenson were already at their stations when Owens jumped in and began the engine starting procedure. The engine whined, the blades turned, the chopper lifted off. Owens climbed only to fifty feet and leveled off, turning left as he did.

Airborne for only a minute, the Huey was struck several times by .50 caliber shells, some striking the control cables. The Huey snap rolled and plunged into the ground inverted, exploding on impact. Rockets and machine gun rounds exploded adding to the fire of the jet fuel. There were no survivors.

OOO

Forty-three years later a classmate from Notre Dame tried to describe in a story a man of such exceptional talent and humanity. He found himself totally inadequate.

OOO

Since his death there has been a hole in my heart that has never healed.

> Greta Baker Allen
> Curtis Baker's sister

25

Lt. Curtis R. Baker USN
(9 October 1938 – 28 March 1967)
Notre Dame 1960

VMO-2 Squadron

THREE

STAR SCOPE

Dong Tam, 1969, 9th Inf. Division HQ

L t. Charlie Jager on his first night as sector defense officer was startled by the warning, "Somethin's up, Lieutenant. There's a guy on our perimeter." Jager tried to clear his head and his eyes at the same time. Pointing a small flashlight at the ceiling of the bunker, the man repeated himself, "Somethin's up, Lieutenant."

Jager moved to the front of the bunker which was lined with sandbags. At the observation windows two other men were engaged in conversation, debating whether to fire or not. An M-60 machine gun poked through a framed opening, a long belt of ammunition coiling into an ammo crate on the floor. At an adjacent opening another man with a night vision star scope probed the darkness. Moving aside he quipped, "Take a look, Sir." A moonless night diminished the scope's effectiveness but as Jager peered through it, he caught something – quick, there and then gone in a flash. Whoever it was had his attention, the men weren't imagining. Sappers had tried the camp's defenses before; they often preceded a rocket or mortar attack in the middle of the night and the night was overcast.

He continued his vigil with the star scope. The company commander's briefing had been explicit, "There are no friendlies in your area." Again, there it was, only this time it stopped in full view- a thin Oriental looking man stripped to the waist, a cloth rag wrapped his head. And then quickly gone again.

Jager cranked the telephone to company headquarters. "Orange-two here, do we have any friendlies in front of our position?"

The reply was harsh and to the point. "That's a free-fire zone in front of you, Orange-two. That was in your briefing. Why are you asking?"

"Sir, there's a guy out there and he's stripped to the waist, moving around haphazardly."

"Lieutenant, shoot the son-of-a bitch. No friendlies, got it?"

Jager hung up the phone. He looked again through the star scope. The bogey popped into view, this time wielding a machete. "Looks like he's clearing brush," Jager offered.

"Could be a sapper, Lieutenant," one of the men replied.

"Could be, but he's spending a lot of effort doing other things."

"Should I waste him, Lieutenant? I've got a clear shot?"

"Naw, let's watch him another minute."

As the bogey continued thrashing about the jungle undergrowth the telephone buzzed. "Orange-two here, "answered Jager. "Yes sir, yes sir. A contractor is clearing brush in front of our position. No, we have not fired on him."

Turning to the other men, "It's a contractor clearing brush. Do NOT fire on him."

"I guess you can go back to sleep, Lieutenant," and then he laughed, "That contractor almost went to sleep for good. I could have hit him five different times but you said NO."

"Yeah, I said NO. That's what they pay me the big bucks for, making decisions."

Jager thought a minute and then added, "If we had killed

him would the captain admit or remember telling me that there were no friendlies out there?" The men laughed in unison. A voice hollered from the next bunker, "Keep it down over there, for Christ sake."

OOO

Lt. Charles Jager never killed a man that he could say for sure. He was a signal officer; other men did the shooting. Many times in the years after the war he recalled the bogey in the jungle. "That would have bothered me for a life time if I'd been hasty. Without the star-scope we probably would have sprayed the area with machine guns and killed the poor old contractor and all the imaginary sappers that didn't exist. Sparing one innocent life was more important then killing a hundred bad guys. I really believe that."

As an after thought he added, "My first day at Dong Tam I saw a bunch of little kids playing at the front gate. Above them, wired to the top of a power pole, was a VC body with half its head blown off. The kids tossed the ball around like everything was jake. I still think about those kids- wonder how they fared when we left. Then too, there are my communication buddies Paul Hurt and Ed Goshorn, both killed by a mine. What a terrible waste."

29

Lt. Charles W. Jager, Co B 52nd/39th Sig Bn (later 327th Sig Co), returning from Ben Tre to base at Dong Tam circa Mar 1969
At ferry from Ben Tre to My Tho, these boys begged Lt. Jager for a ride. Many VC popluated this area, but Jager could not
resist the excited pleas of these kids.   All Rights Owner CWJager grants permission to Dan Rapp to reprint this photo

Lt. Charles W. Jager
Clemson University 1967

Constructing the second radio tower at Lai Khe - I had a single mission honor to command an extraordinarily dedicated team that built this tower. I regret that I cannot remember their names, but their exemplary pride and passion to "get-it-done" still inspire me to this day. 6-11-1969

327th Signal Company (Microwave/Troposcatter)
Lai Khe Tower #2 Construction, circa June 11, 1969

Maybe his name was "Red." Can't remember. But, I have never forgotten his response when I said, "Don't climb outside the tower. I don't want to scrape you up and send you and my letter to your family." He said, "Sir, we need to get this tower built fast. I work faster outside the tower." I let him go and I asked God to protect him.

Lt. Charles W. Jager, 327th Sig Co

Lt. Jager (far right) and his men prepare to raise TRC-97 antenna onto tower at Dong Tam, 1969

Lt. Jager prepares to leave Dong Tam to inspect remote sites.

9th Infantry Division

FOUR

OUR ALLY

Laos 1969,

R
aven forward air controllers were at their wits end trying to eliminate a pesky North Vietnamese 37mm anti-aircraft gun. Situated at the base of a steep mountain it had 180 degree swing and its heavy shells imperiled any USAF fighter bomber that tried to approach it. F-100's and then the latest F-4 Phantoms tried their best, it was impossible.

"Raven-four, to Tiger-one. Are you in the area thirty kilometers east of Long Tieng? Over!"

The controller's radio crackled with static, "This is Tiger-one. I am south of your position. I am armed and ready, Raven-four. Over."

"I have a large caliber AA gun against the mountain on the west side. I am circling out of range. Over."

'I see you Raven-four. A moment of silence followed, "Ah ha! I see your target Raven-four. Give me a minute. Over."

Raven-four watched as the T-28D flew east passed the steep mountain and then executed a one-hundred-eighty degree turn. Just above the flattened peak of the mountain the Hmong pilot rolled inverted. Once clear of the mountain side he pulled back on the stick until he was flying vertically, heading straight for *terra firma*. The aircraft, rolling a half roll so that its underside faced the mountain, plummeted towards the gun. At three thousand feet he loosed two 250lb. bombs and pulled up in a four-G maneuver. As his eyes cleared the tunnel vision of the pull out, the bombs exploded on the gun. The T-28 then flew south from where it had come.

Amazed by the airmanship he had just witnessed, the flight leader of the circling Phantoms exclaimed, "Who was that masked man?"

OOO

The masked man in question was a former school teacher from Phou Pheng. With six months of training he went to war against the Communists and never rested. In three years he flew over 5,000 sorties. While wearing out twelve T-28D aircraft, he became a legend not only in the Royal Lao Air Force but in the American Air Force. He was Capt. Lee Leu.

In what became known as the Secret War in Laos and Cambodia a generation of men disappeared from the Hmong people. At the end, their army consisted of twelve to fifteen year olds, no taller than the antiquated rifles they carried. Lee Leu lived up to his motto, "Fly 'til you die." He was killed on July 12, 1969 near Muong Suoi.

As the U.S. Government repeatedly denied involvement in the Secret War, a flood of Hmong immigrants escaped to Thailand. With the reversal of policy of the Bush Administration, acknowledgement of the heroic efforts of the American and Hmong fighters became a reality. A memorial was allowed to be constructed at Arlington National Cemetery. Immigration rights to our Hmong allies were opened after lengthy debate. The memorial at Arlington reads as follows:

Dedicated to:
The U.S. Secret Army
In the Kingdom of Laos
1961 – 1973
In memory of the Hmong and Laos combat
veterans and their American advisors
who served freedom's causes in
Southeast Asia. Their patriotic valor
and loyalty in the defense of liberty and
democracy will never be forgotten.
-Laos Veterans of America
May 15, 1997

Maj. Lee Lue, Royal Lao Air Force (1935 – 1969)

FIVE

CRONKITE & TET

Walter Cronkite Jr. (1916-2009) the TV anchorman for more than thirty years won many awards for journalism and TV reporting. After the Tet Offensive by North Vietnam and their Viet Cong allies he reported this, *"It is increasingly clear that the only rational way out will be to negotiate, not as victors but as an honorable people who lived up to the pledge to defend democracy."*

President Lyndon Johnson responded: "If I've lost Cronkite, I've lost Middle America." Would the perception be so negative if Cronkite had reported the six thousand priests, teachers, students, nurses and doctors murdered by the Viet Cong in Hue? Would the American people have sunk into despair if Cronkite reported the tactical victory- 45,000 enemy dead in Tet?

With his narrow view of the battle field and ignorant of the political scene in North Vietnam, Walter Cronkite condemned to death a noble cause in the War against global Communism.

In his report to Ho Chi Minh, General Giap had thought the Tet Offensive was a colossal failure. Intelligence had failed to notify him that 15 battalions of Americans had been moved east to the Saigon area. He was stunned to learn how quickly the Americans responded to the attacks. The American air power pounded his withdrawing troops for weeks. In the end, he lost 45,000 troops. All that Cronkite knew was that a police captain shot a Viet Cong assassin without a trial. It was in an issue of LIFE magazine. Our embassy was attacked by VC. That was played up on the TV for weeks and yet not one of the attackers got into the embassy building. All were dead in thirty minutes.

General Giap began getting the feed-back from America's media. He concluded that Tet was a psychological victory. Ho Chi Minh was pleased.

Giap knew that their war debts to China and the Soviet Union were long over due, the air defense was down to a handful of SAM's, and the air force nearly gone. In his memoirs he concluded that Ho had won the war by a matter of days.

Media members hailed Cronkite's statement as courageous and credited him with saving thousands of lives. There may be some truth to it- at least American lives, but the liberal left turned a blind eye to the carnage that followed in South East Asia.

In Cambodia two million people died at the hands of Pol Pot and his Khmer Rouge, an organization that did not exist before the war ended in Vietnam. A half million died in Laos at the hands of the Pathet Lao, and, as if the South Vietnamese hadn't suffered enough, another 100,000 died in re-education camps and in boat people escape attempts.

Walter Cronkite stepped through the invisible veil when he stopped being a journalist reporting the war and became a political analyst. With limited knowledge of the enemy's position he decided the war a loss. His declaration shocked President Johnson and provoked Congress into defunding the war effort. His stature as a reporter allowed him the latitude of an analyst. "*And that's the way it was-*" Only it wasn't.

They called it the "Domino Theory," where one nation

topples into its neighbor and then the neighbor falls too. They say it never happened, but even a liberal Hollywood could make a movie called "The Killing Fields." Laos and Cambodia were the Dominoes that never fell after Vietnam but the reign of terror lasted two decades.

America was not defeated on the battle field; it was defeated in academia and the media and by protesters who never held a job or shouldered a responsibility and by Walter Cronkite who "only expressed his opinion." Would he have been so well received if he had reported WWII the same way? If he had been at Bastogne in December of '44 or on Okinawa in April of '45 would he have pushed for a negotiated peace when the carnage was even greater? – The enemies even more powerful?

Nam is the legacy of my generation but the heroism and the courage there was every bit as common as in either of the Great Wars. The difference was in the people at home and it showed. Our men came home without ticker tape parades, without welcome and without appreciation. And I ask, "Who was it that sent them there in the first place?"

When Saigon fell, the Communist Party political grandees sprinted down Armond Street to claim the finest homes for themselves. After all that sacrifice of blood and treasure the Vietnamese People were left with nothing. Promised everything from land reform to free election, to social equality, they still have nothing. They're Communists.

In Washington, D.C. we have the Vietnam Wall that reminds us of the 58,000 Americans who died there. Some call it the "Healing Wall" but for others the pain will never heal.

Walter Cronkite Jr.
1916-2009
"And that's the way it was."
-only it wasn't!

Six

BIG BRASS ONES

Korat, Thailand- 11 May, 1972

The Wild Weasels had a difficult and dangerous job to perform, attracting anti aircraft batteries to themselves so they could destroy them. With their F-105G "Thud" Majors Jim Padgett (electronics warfare officer) and Bill Talley (pilot) had flown north twelve times. This was their thirteenth mission.

Padgett worried about the low cloud cover over Hanoi and the handful of Mig's that still prowled the corridor around the city. SA-2 missiles, 21 feet long, still showed on his scanner frequently. The North Vietnamese defense battalions weren't out of ammo yet.

The F-105 roared down the runway and lifted off, after burner blazing. Ground crews smirked at the name painted on the nose of the powerful aircraft, *Big Brass Ones.*

Southwest of Hanoi the warnings went off- bells, buzzers, red light, amber lights, the whole catastrophe. "Six comin'at us in a spread, Calgon." Padgett said calmly into the intercom. In his Southern drawl he mapped the approach angles to his pilot. The Thud yanked him to the left, to the right, the g-forces pressing him to the seat.

The long series of evasive maneuvers seemed to have foiled the SAM's. Seconds later a flash and a loud explosion erupted just below the tail assembly. A Mig-21, piloted by Ngo Duy Thu, had burst from the cloud bank and fired a R3-S missile from their six o'clock position.

As the Thud nosed over, Padgett made a momentous decision, *I don't want to be a prisoner. I'll ride this thing into the ground.* Pilot Bill Talley had other ideas; he released the arm safety covering a red switch. Without warning Padgett's canopy left the aircraft, his seat charge exploded. He felt the air blast hit him from head to foot.

His parachute opened immediately after and he floated lazily towards a rice patty.

Below he could see North Vietnamese farmers scurrying about. To the west Talley's parachute deployed.

Padgett splashed down in the patty, the villagers already advancing towards him.

This is going to be a bad experience. I didn't know Talley could do that.

Getting shot down was a bad experience but things were about to get worse for Padgett and Talley and they both knew it. Other Air Force pilots circling above witnessed the safe parachute landings and the hostile villagers of Phu Xuan.

As Padgett released his parachute harness he thought - *Oh my God. How will Grace and the kids handle this?*

In a minute he was surrounded by villagers with an assortment of clubs, pitch forks and two rusty old rifles. An old man with a gray beard stepped forward, "You prisoner."

"Yeah. Me prisoner." The discomfort of a wet flying suit never entered his mind. Mud dripped down his face. He tried to wipe his hands clean but he couldn't. A skinny hand and arm removed his sidearm and holster. *Helpless* doesn't describe it. Being captured by the enemy starts with a hallow feeling, it's hard to describe. Nothing in his training, not even survival school, prepared him for this. If you have a connection to a Higher Being, it's a good time to call on Him. Jim Padgett would have rather "ridden it into the ground."

OOO

23 June, 1972

North Vietnam acknowledged that Padgett and Talley were on the list of prisoners of war (POW's) held by them. Grace Padgett and her kids welcomed the admission, but the prayers had only begun.

An organization dedicated to the release of POW's began distributing engraved bracelets with names and dates. "MAJOR JAMES PADGETT 5-11-72." A thousand names, ten thousand bracelets spread across the nation. The message was clear, "**Do not abandon these men.**"

The TV Morning Show aired a film strip from one of the prisons north of Hanoi. Clearly framed in the center of the film stood Major James Padgett wearing a prison uniform. Friends in Syracuse, Grace's hometown, hurried to phone her.

While the two sides met almost daily in Paris, President Richard Nixon sent the B-52's to Hanoi. In the Hanoi Hilton, the nickname for the Hoa Lo Prison, more than five hundred POW's cheered as the rumble of bombs shook the night.

Nixon's only trump card was being played like a pro. The SAM's were almost gone from Ho's arsenal. In one night 150 bombers and fighter bombers lost weight over the Hanoi-Haiphong area and not a single SAM was fired. The negotiators in Paris finally relented. They would release the "air pirates."

12 February,1973, under Operation Homecoming, James P. Padgett was repatriated to his country. After being honored by his alma mater at the University of Florida he released an open letter to the press.

This is a special message to all my friends throughout the United

States who shared with my family your concerns for my life and health while I was held captive and who wish to me the best in life after my return and repatriation to my friends and loved ones. Your prayers for us while we were away were heard and our nation was guided to a solution to the conflict by decisive action taken by our government. I am thankful to you for your faith and devotion to our country and to its leader. Please accept my thanks to you for your great concern and comfort for my family in their time of need. I am forever grateful.

Oh, welcome back, ye prisoners!
Home to our waiting arms!
Rush to us, all ye who survived
War's endless brutal harms!
- Harry Dee

Lt. Col James P. Padgett
University of Florida 1955

17th Wild Weasel Squadron

Big Brass Ones - *by Keith Ferris*

Seven

His Lonely War

LIFE Magazine, May 8, 1964

But Captain Shank was also a lonely father trying to keep up the bonds with his family. Above all, he was a dedicated soldier who believed that his frustrating war had to be fought - and that the American people did not know enough or care enough about it.

OOO

He called himself a multi-engine guy but found himself in Vietnam flying single engine T-28 training planes in combat. Jerry Shank's wife Connie had three kids and one on the way, so the separation weighed heavily upon both of them. Winimac, Indiana was a long way away.

Telling his story would only be conjecture, an estimate of how things were in the early stages of the war. But his letters tell it better. Homesick, in danger on a daily basis and disappointed in the support from home, he watched the ill-equipped Air Force falling apart and Americans were being killed while it did.

OOO

14 Nov 63

Dear Connie and Kids

Up to 12 missions now. All checked out for night work and I'm second up for alert tonight. Had another 3 hr. flight. This morning. We escorted choppers back and forth to a landing zone where they put troops in the field. Then we went over and struck some suspicious areas.

We're using equipment and bombs from WWII and it's not too reliable. There are only about 6 maintenance men, 6 armament men and 11 pilots down here. We 23 run the whole T-28 war in the Mekong Delta. This will give you some idea of Uncle Sam's part in the war. I goofed on my third mission out here. I told you we had a real short runway. One approach is over trees and bushes and a couple barbed wire fences. There is only one barbed wire fence now. I brought about 20 ft. of fence home with me.

23 Nov 63

Been real busy with the armament job. Got all kinds of problems-can't get parts or books or charts describing the different bombs and systems. The Air Force hasn't used any of this equipment since Korea, and everybody seems to have lost the books. Main problem is personnel- no good officers or NCOs over here that really know their business. Most of them are out of SAC and have dealt with nuclear weapons. This doesn't apply over here. What we need is someone from WWII. Some days it's like beating your head against a brick wall.

27 Nov 63

Happy Thanksgiving- no different here than any other day. You know damn well where I'd like to be today.

First of all woke up Saturday to the news of Kennedy's assassination. Such a terrible thing- the world is full of animals. Sunday all hell broke loose with the Vietcong. We had a big airborne operation against them- both choppers and parachutes. I'm up to 20 missions now and am real confident in myself. I feel like a veteran. I think I am older.

Although this is called a dirty little war and is far from the shores of the old USA, it's a big mean war. We are getting beat. We are under manned and under gunned. The US may say they are in this, but they don't know. If the US would really put some combat troops in here, we could win and win fast.

4 Dec 63

It's about 9:30- I guess, broke my watch. But I'll get it fixed next time into Saigon. Got my toe rot healed up and also my spider bite. I'm fully operational now.

I have debated for a week and a half now over telling you about Black Sunday- Nov. 24, 1963. I'm going to tell you, and if you don't want to hear about these things again, well say so. You do have a right to know. Anyway, here is what I saw.

At 4:30 Frank Gerski and I took off after a fort under attack. Our airborne interpreter was very poor. The first target he said to hit was an area about the size of your dad's farm. Well, this is much too large a target, but it's all we had. After the first two bombs, we spotted the bad guys shooting at us. So Frank directed me in and I burned them with napalm. Then I spotted another bunch shooting great big bullets at me, so I told Frank to follow me in and shoot where I shot. Well, just as I had them in my gun sights my damn guns jammed. By now, dawn had broken. We were out of goodies and gas, so we came home, landing at around 0700.

We then got word that a big airlift was taking place. Four of our T-28 birds went out- 2 to escort the choppers and 2 to soften up the landing zone. They came home about 2 hrs later- said it was pretty hot. 2 more birds took off to do the same thing for the second wave of choppers. 11/2 hrs later they came home screaming "battle damage." Just after the hurt birds landed two more took off- almost. I watched the first go, then waited for the second. But he didn't make it

His engine quit just at take off. Since the runway's short he didn't have time to stop. Hit a hidden hole and tore a gear off. So now we're down to 2planes out of 6 and it's my turn. We bombed like no one has ever bombed before- we literally obliterated about 600 acres of

Vietcong woods and then came home.

The Vietcong hurt us bad. What they had done was pull into the little village and commit their usual atrocities. Headquarters thought they would teach this little group of Vietcong a lesson. But the crafty little bastards withdrew from the town and into foxholes and bunkers they had been secretly building all week.

So when the first wave went in- thinking it was a routine chase of Vietcong- they soon ran against a Vietcong wall.

*We were lucky. No pilot received so much as a hang nail. We have a tremendous esprit and we are all skilled- so you can be proud of us. I am. There are no heroes over here, but there are a lot of fine men. America better not let us down. **We've got to get in all the way or get out.** If we get out, the Vietcong will be in Saigon the next day.*

I wouldn't read this to the kids. They might not understand. You can understand now why I have a duty over here, why it's a serious duty and no one could possibly shirk it. I believe in our cause- it's just. We must win.

24 March 64

Two days after writing his last letter home, Captain Jerry Shank wasn't shot down by hostile fire, under the weight of the bomb load, the AT-28's wings buckled. Both he and his Vietnamese cadet, Tu Le Trung, were killed.

If Dr. Tom Dooley was the first face of America in the Vietnam War, Captain Jerry Shank was the second. His images and letters in that issue of LIFE Magazine should have stuck in the psyche of America but they didn't. He fought his lonely war far from his family and feeling abandon by his country. America no longer can sustain a long war, and politics plays too large a role.

Was Jerry Shank in the Drill Hall for Tom Dooley's speech? Probably!

Captain Edwin G. Shank (1936- 1964)
Notre Dame 1959

EIGHT
FRATRICIDE

September, 1966

He was 6'0" and very muscular. Classmates called him "Barbell." If you pictured JJ Carroll in your mind, he would be smiling a toothy grin. He was on the college swim team but a diver, not a swimmer.

At GTMO (now called Gitmo, but there is no "I" in Guantanamo) in his early Marine Corps service he delighted fellow Marines with his platform tower diving. JJ was a fun guy to be around, but he was all business when it came to being a Marine.

Just before shipping out for Vietnam he told a friend he was eager to go do what he had trained so hard to do, lead Marines in combat. Within a couple months he was into it as deep as it gets. In Quang Tri Province he was engaged in battle against the North Vietnamese Army's (NVA) 324B Division.

Operation Prairie was conducted in hilly terrain just south of the Demilitarized Zone (DMZ) so the code name was deceiving. 324B threatened the populated coastal region; Operation Prairie was intended to thwart it.

Lyndon Baines Johnson would sign his posthumous Navy Cross Citation and the citation describes JJ Carroll's courage and dedication.

The President of the United States takes pleasure in presenting the Navy Cross to Captain James Joseph Carroll, United States Marine Corps for service as set forth in the following citation:

For extraordinary heroism as Commanding Officer of Company K, third Battalion, Fourth Marines, Third Marine Division in action against North Vietnamese Army forces during Operation PRAIRIE in the Republic of Vietnam from 27 September to 5 October, 1966. On 27 September as Company K moved through a thick jungle canopy toward hill400, the point platoon was hit hard by enemy automatic weapons fire, electrically detonated mines and booby traps, and the other platoons of the company came under intense mortar attack. Captain Carroll quickly seized a piece of high ground, and utilizing it for a temporary landing zone was able to evacuate his wounded quickly and establish a company defensive position from which he could attack the determined and well-fortified enemy bunkers that defended Hill 400. On 28 September, he called in close air support to within fifty meters of his front lines in an attempt to destroy the enemy positions that halted the Battalion for two days. Utilizing the shock action of bombs and napalm, Captain Carroll and seven of his Marines crawled to within hand-grenade range of the enemy. Aggressively and decisively launching the final assault and gaining a quick foothold on the hill, he employed the rest of his company to aid in securing the objective then under heavy counterattack from three sides. Despite a painful wound from an enemy mortar round, Captain Carroll continued to direct his men in the securing of the hill. On 5 October, while directing supporting fire from Company M, he was mortally wounded by an exploding shell fragment. His courageous fighting spirit, great personal valor and unswerving devotion to duty served to inspire all who observed him and were in keeping with the highest traditions of the United States Marine Corps and the United States Naval Service. He gallantly gave his life for his country.

The citation does not tell the whole story of what really happened. During daylight hours Carroll took responsibility for sighting in the guns on the three tanks which covered the valley through which he expected the enemy to attack. He then took himself and his company headquarters to the closest possible position near the valley.

After darkness had fallen two additional tanks were brought up for support. Their aiming points were off by several meters. In the confusion of the ensuing battle an errant 90mm round ripped into the headquarters position mortally wounding Captain Carroll. Fratricide is as old as the Greek hoplites but is still as lethal.

In the War in Vietnam, Air Force pilots mistakenly shot-down their own planes. Army artillery struck trees above our positions with deadly effect and fratricide haunted us just as it did the ancient Greeks. Despite optical and radar controlled sights, night vision star scopes and all of the technology of modern warfare, the human element squeezed into the equation and killed JJ Carroll.

James J Carroll at age 3-1/2 ... always a Marine.

Capt. James J. Carroll
Notre Dame 1959

The Navy Cross

3rd Battalion 4th Marines

NINE

MIG-CAP GOPHER

June 6, 1972, Udorn AFB, Thailand

The 523rd Tactical Fighter Squadron had a new skipper. Maj. James A. Fowler had been around, one hundred missions in F-105's, the highest grade point average ever achieved at the Nellis F-100 school and an abundance of positive intangibles that formulates leadership.

Born in Minnesota in 1938, he had stars in his courses. Already on the promotion list for lieutenant colonel, he had twelve missions towards his second hundred, this time in the new F-4D Phantom.

The day's mission was to protect B-52's on a raid near Hanoi. They called them Mig-cap's. With the call sign "Gopher One," Jim Fowler and three other two man ships headed for the Yen Bai Airfield northwest of Hanoi.

After the B-52's completed their mission, the Phantoms began their trip home. Shortly thereafter, Captain John Seuell, the electronics warfare officer (WSO), alerted the flight that SA-2 anti-aircraft missiles were being fired at them.

The three flight members took immediate action. Gopher

One, waiting a split second for the others to clear, was struck in the rear fuselage by a missile. The Phantom caught fire immediately and crashed. No canopies and no parachutes were observed by the other crews.

The North Vietnamese 261st SAM Regiment reported in an intercepted radio message that both pilots had been killed. But some doubts persisted. The Air Force finally concluded on 6 September, 1979 that the two men were dead and their listing was changed from *Missing in Action* to *Killed in Action*.

For seven years Jim Fowler's wife and mother fought for a clearer explanation of the incident, none was forthcoming. Fowler's and Seuell's remains were never returned by the North Vietnamese Government. Resolution of their deaths was forever denied the families.

F-4 Phantom fighter

Lt. Col. James A. Fowler
Notre Dame 1959

523rd Tactical fighter Squadron

Senior Master Sergeant Mike Yates, 2008:

I had the honor of serving with Maj. Fowler for almost 3 years at Nellis AFB in Nevada working the Red Flame and Pave Fire Projects, and then at Clark Air Base in the Philippines where we were subsequently deployed to Udorn Royal Thai Air Base in Thailand in early 1972. I was a very young 21 year old enlisted guy who worked ground maintenance at the time. Maj. Fowler's F-4 took off mid-morning on June 6th, 1972 on a MIGCAP mission over North Vietnam. When Maj. Fowler's aircraft did not return from his mission, I went to his billet to check on him. The officer who I spoke with told me that he took a SAM missile up the tail of his F-4. He said no parachutes were seen ejecting from the aircraft, and Maj. Fowler and his back-seater, Capt. John Seuell, whom I did not know, were subsequently listed MIA. Maj. Fowler was promoted to Lt. Col., and was listed as KIA September 6, 1979.

On a personal note, to say I was personally devastated at the time is an understatement. I have carried Maj. Fowler with me, so to speak, from then until now, 36 years. In addition, throughout my career in the Air Force, where I served 25 years, I have avoided visiting either the Vietnam memorial or the Moving Wall Memorial until last year, when I thought I could handle it. I was wrong. I cried like a baby, and my wife, who was with me, told me that was the first time she had ever seen me cry. I had never shared this story with her, or anyone else for that matter, until then.

Ten
Wounded in Lima 3/9

2010 Las Vegas, Nevada

Steve Weber of Evanston, IL didn't like to think about the war but his longest day came back to mind at a Marine reunion.

We were walking for about four hours in deep vegetation and just outside the tree line. When the shooting started I dove for cover in a shallow swale off to the left- I took two bullets right away. As if that wasn't enough, a bright flash put heat all over me. It was really loud and I couldn't hear nothin' for a couple minutes. A mortar round landed right next to me. I looked at my left side and it was all peppered full of holes with blood comin' out of them. When I pulled up my flack jacket, I saw a part of my intestine sticking out. I had been thrown about twenty feet from the swale I counted on for cover.

I really felt all alone. Marines were running all over and I wasn't sure anyone even knew I was there. Just about the time I was resigning myself to dying right there, two Marines grabbed me by the shoulders - one on each side. They were dragging me so all I could see were my feet. It's strange but at the time I was worried about where my weapon was. I did not want the enemy to have my M-16 even if I wasn't there to use it.

The further they dragged me, the more confidence I got that I might live through it all. I never saw the faces of those two men but someday I'll know who they were. I think they were from another platoon.

I passed out for a while and then I was being tossed into a helicopter without a lot of tenderness. It was hectic and I had company going in the CH-34. This corpsman was working frantically patching guys up. He looked at me and cut some clothing away. As the chopper lifted off it banked sharply. I started rolling to the open doorway. The crew chief stuck his leg out to stop me but never stopped firing his M-60.

I tell you something- I think I was near death cuz I was like hovering above the helicopter and I could see the whole battle field, Marines running and even saw the NVA in there holes and bunkers- weird. I passed out again, but just enough so I couldn't see. I could hear people talking but they might as well been talking Greek, I couldn't understand anything. That's when I thought, "Dying ain't so bad- shoot." Yeah it hurts, but I've seen other guys in bad pain but it wasn't that way. I think God took pity on me.

About then I did hear someone say, "That one's got his guts held in with the big safety pins." I assumed he was talking about me and that scared me a bunch."

I tried real hard to see the corpsman's face but I couldn't. Then I tried to see the pilot's face and I couldn't. He had sun glasses and a microphone holder in front of his face. Every thing and everyone got blurry. I thought I must be losing blood real fast, and then I passed out all the way.

The next thing I knew I was in a dispensary or hospital thing in Dong Ha and a priest was giving me the last rights of the Church. I was wrapped in a body bag- not a confidence boost. Then a nurse with a green mask was kneeling next to me. She said, "We've got you covered, Marine. You're going to be all right. She had pretty brown eyes and that's all I could see of her. I wanted to thank her for being there, but I couldn't talk. I could hardly breathe.

I went into surgery and someone put an anesthesia mask over my face. Someone said, "Count backwards, Marine, starting with ten." I couldn't. I had a bad head ache and then I went under.

...And now I look back on it and think about all those people who did what they did to save my life, the two Marines, the corpsman in the chopper, the nurse, the doctors. They were all in danger ya know. Just being over there, they were in danger.

It chokes me up to think about them, yeah, me the hard ass Marine with all the shrapnel. I'm sixty-three now; my kids think I am a direct descendant of Attila the Hun. One of my grand kids calls me "Vlad the Impaler." But really, I'm a big softy. War does that to a person.

I use to see the old vets from WWII and Korea marching in the Memorial Day and 4th of July parades. Now "they" is "us."

Oh! One more thing, yesterday at this reunion, a guy came up to me and said, "You probably don't remember me, but I remember you. You saved my ass a few days before you got hit." I said, "What did I do?" He got all choked up and tried to hide the tears. I said, "Semper Fi- buddy." I hugged him like a brother, but then, he is a brother.

Steve Weber mans M-60 machine gun with unidentified assistant.

The Purple Heart

Semper Fidelis

ELEVEN

MISTY 13

26 Aug. 1967 Phu Cat, South Vietnam

Captain Corwin "Kipp" Kippenhan was the thirteenth volunteer to sign up for the new fast forward air controller squadron. George "Bud" Day, Misty Squadron CO, had a new theory on forward air controllers and a personal magnetism to attract his kind of pilots.

Kipp had flown as a slow forward air controller O-1 as a covey FAC and as the back seat in the F-100F fast forward air control. Today was his opportunity to get upgraded to the front seat job for he had originally been trained as a pilot in the F-100.

This should be a training mission, right? Not so- the upgrade would take place north of the DMZ where intelligence had info the enemy was bringing in SA-2 anti-aircraft missiles. This was bad news for the B-52's that frequently pounded the enemy build-up there.

Near an area of the Fingers Lake, they met intense anti-aircraft fire, heavy stuff like 37mm. One pass through that maelstrom was enough. They headed to another location and then out over the Gulf of Tonkin for a refueling rendezvous. Maybe the gunners at the Fingers Lake would relax while they were gone.

As Kipp made his second pass the gunners began their barrage. Despite it Kipp spotted the SAM. "I've got it in sight," he exclaimed into the mask microphone. Bud Day insisted on a third pass to positively identify the target. As they did a cannon shell exploded in the tail and they lost control.

Bud Day ejected first and Kipp right after him. As Kipp floated in the parachute he could see that the high speed ejection had torn two panels out of his chute. He thought he was falling too fast when he saw Bud Day pass him on the way to the ground. Bud was in for a rough landing.

Search and Rescue forces went into action immediately and a Jolly Green Giant helicopter from HH-3 homed in on Kipp's beeper and then his rescue radio instructions. Fortunately for Kipp he was picked up quickly by Ray Dunn and Rich Blackwell. For HH-3 he was their ninety-fifth rescue. But Bud Day was lost in the jungles and rough terrain north of the DMZ.

Early the next morning the search was renewed. Surrounded by North Vietnamese soldiers Bud could not signal the chopper for help. So close and yet so far- Bud could see someone in the chopper's doorway with an M-16 rifle in his hands. Two hundred yards or so and it was too far. The chopper broke away instead of towards him.

The search went on for several days but was called off when no more signals came from Bud's beeper. He was on his own, badly injured from the bailout, hungry, thirsty, and physically exhausted. But the worst was yet to come for Bud Day. His capture, escape and recapture are recorded in the book "Bury Us Upside Down," by Rick Newman and Don Shepperd.

Bud Day's harsh treatment at the hands of his North Vietnamese captors was met with defiance. His defiance met with torture and beatings. After five and a half years of it Bud was repatriated on 17 March, 1973.

His exploits and subsequent Medal of Honor award are covered in the book "American Patriot" by Robert Coram. Nobody wrote a book about Corwin Kippenhan. After the shoot-down Kipp went to Hawaii to see his wife Josette.

Upon his departure from Hawaii he was promised a slot in an F-100 squadron which is what he had been trained to fly. Back in Vietnam the promise quickly disappeared. The choices left him were: A.) go back to his old squadron (20th Tactical Support Squadron) and the O-2A aircraft or B) fly the back seat of an F-100F. Front seat options were closed.

He chose his old unit based at Da Nang and was once again a covey forward air controller pilot. Much fighting soon followed. One operation sticks out in Kipp's memory as much as his shoot-down with Bud Day.

8 Nov 1967, Laos

After supervising the insertion of an SOG team (Studies and Observation Group), Kipp got radio reports that the team had come under attack. With only twelve men (NCO's and Montagnard mercenaries), they could not fend off the much larger enemy force. The team leader was blinded by enemy fire, and Kipp called to headquarters for an extraction helicopter. His request was refused at 10:00. Twelve hours later headquarters changed their mind.

The ensuing snafu left three helicopters shot down, another shot up so it never flew again and six good men were dead. A total of seventeen other men had to be rescued by further courageous efforts. The operation dragged out for three days and several night operations, involving gun ship helicopters, a C-130 Puff the Magic Dragon and a ground force rescue team. One helicopter pilot was awarded the Medal of Honor, Capt. Gerald O. Young and a second the Air Force Cross, Capt. John McTasney.

"I was pissed," Kipp said after recounting the episode. "I

told the CO if I couldn't call the shots in the field, everyone else could stick it." The CO honored his request and Kipp didn't fly much after that outburst, administration missions only. By then Kipp had flown 275 combat sorties and was less than two months from being rotated back home.

In his career Corwin Kippenhan flew O-1, O-2 (100 missions), F-100 and F-106 aircraft.

OOO

Kipp attends every Misty reunion. He decorates his automobile with Misty-13 decals on the bumper and his front license plate pictures an F-100F with red letters "Hit My Smoke" and black script "Misty13."

Most people would say "Misty-13, that's got to be unlucky," but it was "Misty-1" that was unlucky. Years later Kipp would admit, "I could take being lost in the jungles for a lengthy time. I could deal with it, but I wouldn't have done very well in that North Vietnamese prison. When two guys go out and one comes back, that's not a good deal."

Maybe God spared Kipp the ordeal. Maybe Bud Day had to suffer it in order to lead the others home. Only God knows.

Forty-three years after being shot down and rescued, Kipp still keeps in touch with the helo pilots that rescued him, Ray Dunn and Rick Blackwell. The picture below shows him with the tag that reads, "HH-3 Rescue Squadron #95- STICK WITH ME."

HIT MY SMOKE!

Misty 13

Corwin Kippenhan's Auto License Plate

**Major Corwin Kippenhan with Jolly Green
(U.S. Air Force Academy 1963)**

71

TWELVE

THE PHOTOGRAPH

Saigon, January 31, 1968

I t was called the Tet Nguyen Dan celebration and the Viet
Cong had declared a thirty-six hour cease fire. The lunar
New Year had all the festivities and fire works that it
usually had, but it was generally peaceful until the wee
hours of the morning. The truce ended with the rattle of small
arms and grenade bursts. The Tet Offensive had begun.

Viet Cong assassins arrived at the American embassy in a
truck and a taxi, shooting embassy guards before they knew
they were under attack. A few blocks away other VC dressed in
shorts and sport shirts murdered a National Police officer along
with his wife and children. One of the murderers was captured
by South Vietnamese security forces the following day.

In the furor of the moment General Nguyen Ngoc Loan
exacted his punishment on the skinny infiltrating murderer. He
shot him in the head at close range with the killer's own gun.
An Associated Press photographer named Eddie Adams
snapped the picture at the precise moment of execution. The
photo was the rage of the media for two full weeks and

splashed the pages of LIFE Magazine on February 9th.

The anti-war media cried atrocity, forgetting that the insurgent had just murdered several people and that he wore no military uniform or signature of rank. He was a terrorist. Also forgotten in the media frenzy were the 6,000 priests, doctors and teachers murdered the same day by Viet Cong in Hue. 3000 bodies lay in the streets; another 3000 simply disappeared. A Viet Cong official would later pass it off as the removal of the "unnecessary Bourgeoisie." Other atrocities too numerous to recount touched the length and width of the country, but the media clung to the photograph. Eddie Adams got a Pulitzer.

Camera shots of a few burning homes made it look like the entire city was ablaze. The few Americans slain on the embassy grounds were shown time after time on the evening news. Interviews with war weary Marines and soldiers gave the viewers the impression they'd been whipped, when in fact it was the enemy that had taken the beating.

No cameras were present to show the American air power decimating Communist battalions as they fled north. None showed the artillery raining on them in such amounts and with such accuracy that even Gen. Giap of North Vietnam was amazed.

Instead the Viet Cong murderer was given sympathy because he didn't get a fair trial in a country torn by war since 1941. The VC atrocities got little media play but it found lots to crow about on March 16th when an inexperienced 2nd Lt. named William Calley did what he was told to do. Bullied by his company commander, Capt. Ernest Medina, Calley ordered his men to kill over three hundred Vietnamese villagers at My Lai. The outrage around the world did irreparable damage to the image and morale of the American military. It was only this greater wrong that put the Tet photo into the background.

By then the media had all it needed to prosecute the war itself. Calley served three years of a life sentence. Captain

Medina and his battalion commander were never charged.

Years after the war Gen. Loan was asked if he harbored any ill will towards Eddie Adams. He replied, "No, he had a job to do and I had a job to do."

The Photograph

Eddie Adams (1933-2004)
"I wasn't making a political statement;
I was just reporting the news."

THIRTEEN

SNIPER

Men of the 3rd Battalion 9th Marines carried a bit of psychological warfare with them in the engagements of 1967. A North Vietnamese sniper firing from concealed positions had shot three of their men in three different fights. Each time the sniper chose the third man, not the man on point. It was worrisome to say the least and the problem was never solved.

But the knife cuts both ways and the NVA and VC took their lumps from our snipers. Armed with bolt action rifles with extra heavy barrels, Carlos Hathcock, Eric England, Chuck Mawhinney, and Adelbert Waldron took a heavy toll of the enemy.

It is estimated that Carlos Hathcock killed more than 300 of the enemy although his confirmed kills stood at 93. In his tours of Vietnam Hathcock killed an NVA general (a 700 yd shot), a VC terrorist sniper who tortured captive Marines, a French interrogation officer working for the NVA and an entire platoon of NVA.

The NVA put a bounty on his head like a wild-west desperado- $30,000, and then sent their best sniper to collect it.

In the ensuing gunfight Hathcock killed the enemy sniper after seeing a sun glint from of his scope. The bullet traveled the length of the scope and into the victim's eye… and beyond. The action near Hill 55 was witnessed by his spotter John Burke who retrieved the enemy's damaged scope.

Later reflecting on the incident Carlos concluded that the enemy sniper had drawn a bead on him and that Carlos fired two seconds early or he would have been killed himself.

Hathcock later regretted killing the general because the NVA stepped up their attacks in that sector and other Marines were killed. He reasoned they were punishing the Marines for killing their general. He must have also known he was following orders even if it was a dangerous volunteer mission.

The Corps has many heroes in its history, John Basilone, Chesty Puller, Joe Foss, Pappy Boyington and thousands of others. Included among them is Gunny Sgt. Carlos Hathcock.

OOO

You can watch the interviews of Carlos Hathcock on U-tube. He talks about the most difficult of his many assignments and about the theory of a good sniper. "I never liked the killing, it was my job. I loved the hunting."

The woman sniper who tortured captive Marines, he didn't regret killing. "I shot her, and then I shot her again. That was an evil woman." The Marines nicknamed her Apache Woman.

Carlos Hathcock (1942-1999)

FOURTEEN

AGENT ORANGE

Near the Poka River 1969

Pfc. Donny Brice from Atlanta, Georgia sat exhausted on the barren landing zone. He'd just marched three days through mountainous terrain looking for North Vietnamese regulars. The helicopters were late, it was hot and his clothing was wet with perspiration. He rubbed his nearly bald head, wiping the perspiration with a bandana. With his arms wrapped around his knees he dosed a bit trying to get a second wind.

His rest period ended abruptly when someone said loudly "Ain't that some shit!" When he looked down the mountain slope to the muddy brown river, he saw two Viet Cong riding a makeshift raft, their bodies in the water up to their waists. In the middle of the raft sat a big black plastic bag four feet in diameter.

A fellow trooper took aim and fired three rounds which struck the bag spewing rice upon the water. A sergeant ordered a cease fire, "Use the thump guns. Use the thump guns."

Two men stepped forward and began lobbing the grenades

from the thump guns but the explosions were muffled by the water. White water geysers rose ten feet but the two NVA continued on their way. The sergeant gave up on the thumpers, "Direct your fire on those two men in the water."

The entire platoon was now standing and firing. The bag and the rice splattered everywhere. So did the two men, but they weren't really men, more like teen-agers, skinny dark skinned, shirtless. The bullets tore into them, a few at first and then a fusillade. "Cease fire," yelled the sergeant.

The two NVA floated face down, their blood coloring the brown water red in a big oval. Donny never fired his weapon. Enough others did. *We look for them for three days and don't find a thing and then they float past us like a shooting gallery. They never ducked under water and tried to swim to the bank. What idiots.*

He could hear the choppers in the distance. *If they were on time those two Charley's would have gotten away. To hell with 'em.*

OOO

The warm water felt good even if the makeshift bathtub didn't. He scrubbed himself with a fading bar of Ivory soap. It was then that he first noticed the rainbow patterns on the surface, oily, smelly. *It's that shit they sprayed on us the first day out, the defoliant.* Donny splashed the water with a cupped hand. Part of the oil slick left the tub. He splashed again. A buddy walked up to his bath, a beer in hand. "Want one, Donny?"

"Sure. Got a smoke?"

'Geez, he wants everything. Can I get you a nice fluffy towel?"

"No, just a damn cigarette." His buddy obliged. He tapped the end of the cigarette against the back of his hand, and then leaned into the friends Zippo lighter. "Thanks, Eddy."

"You're welcome, your majesty,"

Donny looked again at the rainbow slick that just wouldn't go away from his bath water. He swigged a sip of beer, puffed

82

on the cigarette. In Nam that was as good as it got.

OOO

1976, Atlanta, Georgia

Donny Brice kick started his Harley Fat Boy. His shoulder length hair flopped beneath his metallic blue helmet as he did. The engine roared. He took the last drag on a cigarette and then flicked it into the gutter. Something wasn't right. The pressure in his arm pit had never been there before. With his finger tips he massaged the area. "What the hell is that," he said as he felt the grape sized lump.

The Harley rumbled down the street, neighbors scowling, staring. They gave him a pass though, never complaining to him or his aging parents. *Donny had gone to war when he was eighteen. We knew he wasn't **just right**.*

When the lump grew to the size of a golf ball Donny went to the VA hospital on Clairmont Rd. "Residue 2,4-D and 2,4,5-T" the doctor repeated. Donny didn't know what the numbers meant. His blank stare prodded the doctor further, "You have Agent Orange, son."

Donny's heart sank. That he did understand. Soft tissue sarcoma and Hodgkins Disease, he understood those too. Nervously, he chewed on his finger nail. "We're going to put you on the sixth floor, son. We want to do more testing." The doctor patted him on the shoulder; a nurse stood at the door. "Agent orange, goddam." The nurse tried to smile but she couldn't.

The longer he stayed, the bigger the lump grew. Worse yet others had been detected by CT scan. Donny slipped into depression. Days later he was moved to the psych ward on the eighth floor.

His mind couldn't leave Vietnam behind and now his body couldn't either. As he stared out the window, "I was too young.

I didn't know who I was yet and I was trained to be a killer and then sprayed with poison."

The doctor sat at the foot of his bed, "How many times were you exposed to it?"

Donny breathed deeply, "Three, maybe four times. I'm not sure. One time I was taking a bath at the fire base and I saw the rainbow floating on the water. I thought it was residue from the barrel."

OOO

Dow, Monsanto and Diamond Alkali made it. The Air force and Army spread it under Operation Ranch Hand and four million Vietnamese were exposed to it. 200,000 of them have some form of sickness attributed to defoliants.

In 1984 a class action suit by former GI's earned a settlement of $180 million. Most men got a lump sum single payment of $1200.

Many mistakes were made in Vietnam which caused loss of life. Agent Orange stands at the top of the list. 12 million gallons fell like the morning dew from the planes and helicopters and just like bombs they maimed and killed…it just took longer.

Donnie Brice died in the VA Hospital in Atlanta a victim of the war. His name is not on the Vietnam Wall in Washington. It should be. He never received a Purple Heart. He should have.

OOO

I do not have a picture of Pfc. Donny Brice but recall with clarity one he showed me. He sat on the bare earth roof of a sand bag bunker, an M-16 rifle in hand, his head shaved nearly bald. With a black felt pen he had written across the bottom of the 8 X 10 color print "Age nineteen."

**C-123 aircraft spray Agent Orange along power lines
between Dalat and Saigon, August 1963**

FIFTEEN

THE SWITCHAROO

S uppose in the fifth inning of a major league baseball game the commissioner came to the dugout and said "Here, try this one." He flipped the manager a Dudley softball, "We're going to this new ball. We think it will work out good."

Well that was the case in the middle of the war in Viet Nam, the Pentagon switched rifles from the M-14 to the M-16. Without training, without spare parts and with a cleaning rod for every fourth one, that's how the M-16 replaced the M-14 rifle, sometimes with catastrophic results. Excerpts are from *A Rifle Company's Tale.*

OOO

From: George D Navadel
To: dan rapp
Sent: Friday, August 06, 2010 10:59 PM
Subject: Nam & the Swtcheroo

Here is the straight skinny on the change over from the M-14 to the M-16. this is a story in itself and is nowhere to be found this explicitly to my knowledge. It is from the troopers' perspective – the guys who had to live with the switch.

Semper Fidelis,
George

Introduction of the New Rifle

GDN (George D. Navadel) – In late March, trucks arrived at the logistic compound at Camp Carroll bringing boxes and boxes of the new M-16 rifles. The shipment came with a lot of misgivings. Marines intimately knew and thoroughly relied on their issued M-14 rifle and its 7.62 cartridges. They were birthed with the weapon at Boot Camp. They earned their marksmanship badges with it at the rifle ranges at Parris Island and Pendleton. The rifle had faithfully stood by them during their present combat tour. Now they were going to be directed to give up something that had been a part of them and adopt, as they would a child, a new fangled, lighter, highly touted weapon that looked like it had been purchased at the toy store in the local home town mall. It took the troopers no time at all to hang a nickname on the new rifle – "Matte Mattel".

See Photo at end of Chapter

The rifle shipment came with a laundry list of NCN's (National Stock Numbers) and rumors of problems from U.S. Army units in Vietnam that had already been equipped with the M-16. (As is always the case, the Doggies got first dibs. In this case it was not a good deal for the soldiers.)

The NSN list came with no noun nomenclature to let the receiving unit know what part or what supporting equipment the number referred to. It was just a long list of numbers. The header notice on the list stated emphatically that no rifle was to be issued until 100% of the list of NSN's was on board. Further, a report of 100% fill was required to be made to higher headquarters and permission given to initiate the weapon swap. This prohibition kept the M-16's on the shelf until the middle of April when all but one of the mystery numbers was aboard. When it was realized by the powers-that-be that the missing item was the cord lanyard to tie the tip of the bayonet scabbard to the rifleman's thigh, the order to issue the new and recover the old was issued.

The S-4 Shop dutifully recovered the tested M-14's and issued the shiny new, lighter M-16's along with the associated lighter, smaller but reportedly more lethal 5.56 ammunition. Although we had heard the new rifle required a lot more care and cleaning to ensure proper and continuous functioning, I was appalled to find that only enough cleaning rods were allocated to provide one for every four rifles. This made me wonder, who back in the States was receiving a cash award for his or her cost saving "Beneficial Suggestion".

The S-3 Shop set up a make shift firing range off to the side of the camp for the companies to use to establish battle sight for each Marine's rifle. (Battle sight was the elevation and windage adjustment each individual marksman set on his personal rifle so he would hit the center of mass of a target at a range of three hundred meters.)

The first combat experience 3d Battalion 9th Marines had with the new weapon was a bad one. While India Company was reorganizing and drawing replacements from within the Battalion and without, Kilo and Mike Companies were placed under the operational control of 3d Battalion 3d Marines after 1st Battalion 9th Marines had been pulled out of the field due to excessive casualties. On 29 and 30 April they were sent up Hill

881 South. After Mike took the initial casualties the first day, they were held near the bottom of the hill while Kilo made the assent and took a hell of a pounding on the 30th. Eventually all Marine dead were recovered. Their equipment, still in the condition in which it was when picked up in the field, was returned to the S-4 (still me at the time) at Camp Carroll for salvage and redistribution.

All the new M-16 rifles were piled in the back of a 6X6 truck. I was sickened by what I saw. The rifle of each dead Marine had the primer end of a live round extending out of the breach. Closer examination revealed two causes for the malfunctions. The most prevalent was double feeding occasioned by too much spring pressure in the twenty round magazine that fed the cartridges to the weapon. This prevented the bolt from going home because it stripped the top two rounds rather than one. The second cause was a ruptured cartridge in the chamber. After the first round was fired, residual carbon caused the brass cartridge to freeze as the extractor on the bolt attempted to draw it out. The following round had no place to go. These men were left defenseless. The firepower of the entire fighting unit was severely curtailed. Kilo Company could not gain fire superiority. Fire superiority belonged to the NVA on Hill 881 South that day.

What happened to a machine gun squad leader on 29 April is typical of what many of the Marines of the battalion experienced on our first major encounter with the NVA since returning to Vietnam from refit and retrain on Okinawa.

Cpl. Jerry Loretta – Machine Gun Squad Leader M/3/9: "My squad was attached to the lead platoon as we started up the lower hills leading up to 881S. We were directly behind the lead squad in a column formation. (None of the squad leaders were happy with not being deployed with more fire power to the front.) The grunt squad just crested the hill when they were hit with accurate fire from the tree line to the left flank. Every man

90

was hit. I deployed my gun team to bring fire into the enemy position to suppress their fire as the dead and wounded were pulled back out of the killing zone by other Marines and Corpsmen."

As soon as the casualties were cleared, I sent my two ammo humpers back to cover while my gunner provided suppressive fire. I then told my gunner to get back as I covered him. My plan was to empty my M-16 magazine into the enemy position in the tree line and dash to cover.

Bang-Bang! Oh Shit!" That was all she wrote. My M-16 jammed – never happened with my M-14. A desperate effort to clear the weapon failed. I moved to get to cover and, not being able to keep the enemy's heads down, I took an AK-47 round in the hip and was out of action.

See Photo at end of chapter

GDN (George D. Navadel)- I thought to myself, "Thank God for that missing bayonet scabbard lanyard!" But for that insignificant piece of cord, India Company could have been armed with the "Matte Mattel" on 30 March.

Cpl. Jack Riley – 2d Platoon: "If you shoot the enemy in the heart – head – neck, in that preferential order, both the M-14 and the M-16 will do nicely! Giving up the tried and true M-14 for the Matte Mattel M-16 was very difficult for me. Yes, we could hump much more ammo plus we could lay down much more suppressive fire but, if a well placed round was not appropriately placed in the aforementioned brain housing group, they kept coming! I can tell you that had my platoon been equipped with that weapon instead of the M-14 on 30 March, me and what was left of my platoon would not have survived Getlin's Corner. The M-16 was and is a deadly weapon but its' .223 cal. Round is no match for the M-14's .308 cal. When it comes to stopping power.

91

GDN – The individual Marine knew he had a problem requiring an immediate fix. There was no time to wait for instructions or permission from on high to make the necessary modifications to gain a semblance of reliability with their new rifle.

The problem of double feeding was partially solved by disassembling each twenty round magazine and cutting off one section of the leaf spring. This lessened the pressure that pushed the rounds to the top of the magazine to be fed into the chamber of the rifle. Even with that the trooper did not dare put more than eighteen rounds in a magazine for fear more would increase the upward pressure and attempt to chamber the top two rounds – a double feed – at the same time.

Ensuring the chamber of the M-16 remained relatively free of carbon and dirt was an extremely difficult task, given the climate and field conditions the rifle was continually subjected to. Besides, a rifleman could not take time out during a skirmish to clean his weapon, particularly when he had to share the cleaning rod. Help came from an unauthorized outside source.

A retired Marine had invented a concoction of graphite and kerosene he called "Dry-Slide". He attempted to sell his lubricant to the DOD (Department of Defense) without success. He sent cases of the stuff to units fighting in Vietnam at his own expense because he knew regular gun oil and lubriplate would not last in the conditions we faced. His "Dry-Slide" on those "Matte Mattels" proved to be a real lifesaver.

It took about two months for the military-industrial complex to rectify their first horrible blunder by not properly field-testing the functioning of the magazines. Corrective action was taken to replace the magazines with fully functional new ones capable of being loaded with the full compliment of twenty rounds.

The supply system finally coughed up more cleaning rods. However, the easily fouling chamber of the M-16 would not be cured until the rifle was finally replaced by the M-16A1 with a chrome-lined chamber. (We would not see the modified rifle on this combat tour.)

The Exchange

T'was March, '67, Ba Long Valley, RVN
My Platoon Sergeant called us together again.
Told us he had something to say,
An old friend will be leaving today.
One who has been with you all the way,
Thru MCRD --- Edsen Range --- ITR,
Always near and never far.
Weather soaked with rain or muddy ground,
Forever dependable, never letting you down.
Always ready to go when time came around.

We gathered at the wire to bid adieu
To the old friend we so intimately knew.
When it came my turn to say goodbye,
Did I detect a slight tear in my eye?
I cursed and complained and caused a real scene,
Because you see ----
The friend who was leaving
Was my M-14.

- Harry Joe O' Dell K 3/9 2d Plat '66-'67 RVN

M-14 Rifle

M-16 Rifle

Cpl. Jerry Loretta

Cpl. Jack Riley

Old Reliable M-14

Chambering a round

Sixteen

CHINA BEACH

I n the spring of 1988 a new TV show hit the tube entitled "China Beach." Sixty-four episodes spanned a four year period telling about the experiences of an Army nurse named Colleen McMurphy. Diana Ross sang the theme song "Reflections."

The setting in a Vietnam hospital weaved a dose of romance intertwined with the demanding job of treating wounded men. With the war then fifteen years in the rear view mirror, the public could face in fiction what it couldn't face every night on the evening TV news.

The lead-in went something like this, "I used to dream about being on a sandy beach surrounded by a bunch of handsome guys. Sometimes you have to watch what you wish for." The story that follows is a composite of four such nurses who at various times told part of their experience.

Lt. Norma Chapman, an Army nurse, thought she would go to someplace like Ft. Sam Houston at San Antonio. Her husband was resigned to a year in Vietnam. They were both wrong. He stayed home and she went to *China Beach.*

OOO

When I arrived in-country, I was amazed at the size of the facility at Chu Lai, a sprawling single story thing that went on forever. It had an amphitheater for USO shows and a helicopter port, a jet base and mess halls and barracks building Quonsets in endless rows.

A sandy beach, with lava rock at one end was a welcome relief if you could overlook the coil of razor ribbon at the dune line or the ogling GI's. Everything else looked like a second level slum carved out of a sparsely grown jungle. Colorless, tasteless but not odorless, the mud stunk, the latrines stunk, the rotting vegetation on the perimeter stunk. There were mud puddles everywhere, some a hundred feet across. I was not a happy camper.

All of that, all the niceties that didn't exist became immaterial when the first casualties came in. I think I experienced what the foot soldiers feel when they first are called to combat. There is something frightening, something terrible about other lives depending on you to do the right thing. My mouth was suddenly dry as cotton, the air was hot but I felt a chill all over my neck and back. I said to myself- **Show time, Norma. Suck it up, girl!** *The helicopters came in two or three at a time, each one carried three maybe four wounded and some were already in body bags.*

I couldn't believe how horrible the wounds looked. Nothing had prepared me for this; intestines outside the stomach cavity, collapsed lungs, head wounds just gushing blood. Everybody worked for ten or eleven very stressful hours. When we finished with the last one, I was told to go get some rest. I staggered back to the barracks and fell on my cot. Buried my face in a thin little pillow and cried. How can I take this for a whole year? I asked myself.

My solitude was interrupted by the voice of the head nurse, "Get it all out, Chapman. You're no different than the rest of us. Right now you're feeling sorry for yourself, not those mangled boys over there. But it's okay. Cry it all out and do it one time. The next time you cry it will be for them and it won't ever stop. Thirty years from now you'll remember the nineteen year old kid that you helped save and then you'll remember one you didn't… couldn't. Oh, one more thing.

Don't let them see you crying. Keep it to yourself."

I took her advice and she was right of course. I still see those wounded boys in dreams occasionally, but mostly in day dreams. Faces without names, so young, I don't know how the brain saves all that stuff.

I remember the first time I saw maggots in a wound. I almost barfed. The surgeon looked over and said,"The surgeon's little helpers eating away the decay."

At Christmas we had a nice service. The chaplain gave a nice sermon about keeping focused on our jobs because so many were depending on us. He examined the corporal works of mercy that we performed on a daily basis and that it was every bit as rewarding as prayer. And then he said God will not forget what you've done here.

Ten months later, when I stepped off the plane back at Hamilton Air Base in California, I didn't expect a parade or bands playing. I remembered what that chaplain said. It was all I needed to come home with. Yeah, I think I did some good over there.

OOO

During the Vietnam War 7,484 women served our country in the Republic of Vietnam. 6,250 of them were nurses. Six nurses were killed in action and one died of a stroke caused by war related stress. One other died of an illness contracted in-country.

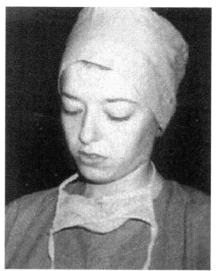

Capt. Eleanor Grace Alexander
(Killed in aircraft accident 30 Nov 67)

2nd Lt Pamela Dorothy Donovan
(Died of rare illness 8 Jul 68)

2nd Lt. Carol Ann Drazba, R.N.
3rd Field Hospital - 4th Med BDE USARV
11 December 1943 - 18 February 1966
Dunmore, Pennsylvania

2nd Lt Carol Ann Drazba
(Killed in helicopter crash 18 Feb 66)

Lt Col Annie Ruth Graham
(Died of stroke while on duty)

2nd Lt Elizabeth Ann Jones
(Killed in helicopter crash 18 Feb 66)

Capt Mary Therese Klinker USAF
(Died in crash of C-5, Op Babylift)

1st Lt Sharon Ann Lane
(Killed by rocket hit on hospital 8 Jun 69)

1st Lt Hedwig Diane Orlowski
(Killed in aircraft accident 30 Nov 67)

On 4 April 1975 a C-5 aircraft crashed after takeoff near Saigon killing 67 American Red Cross nurses and aid workers and USAF nurse Capt. Mary Therese Klinker. Operation Babylift attempted to take 195 Vietnamese orphans out of the country. There were no survivors.

Seventeen

Swift Boats

T hey were like world War II PT boats but different. Different in weapons, they carried no torpedoes, and different in deployment. The Swifties went up river to interdict the enemy's water-borne supply boats, not out to sea to find them.

Traveling in pairs they could cover each other with .50 caliber machine guns and small arms fire. One would approach a sampan or junk, board it and search for weapons, ammunition or other contraband. The second would stand off and cover the first.

As the Swifties prowled the back waters of the Mekong, its Delta and the Dam Doi River, they did so without political motivation. There was a war to be fought and stopping or at least limiting the flow of supplies to the enemy was their mission, and they took it seriously. One in their number did not. Lt Jg John F. Kerry was motivated solely by politics and his own aggrandizement.

It was treasonable, but he met with North Vietnamese officials in Paris anyway, the war still raging. He later testified before Congressional Fullbright Committee that he had personally witnessed atrocities committed by his own unit, Coastal Division 11..."raped, cut off ears, cut off heads, etc, etc, reminiscent of Genghis Kahn."

When asked for specific incidents he could not recall one. Name individuals, he could not. The only one he could have recalled was he himself firing at a man on a sampan without correct interpretation of the meaning "free fire zone."

While Kerry pursued Silver and Bronze Stars and three Purple Hearts with fraudulent applications, his fellow Swifties cringed. Later they uncovered three applications for one award made by three different men and each with a different account of what happened. His Purple Hearts were questionable too. One wound "no worse than a rose thorn would inflict," said one fellow officer. Another was self inflicted, not by enemy fire, but by his own improper handling of a grenade launcher.

By the time Senator John Kerry (D- MA) was campaigning for the 2004 presidential election, the Swifties had a book, "Unfit for Command," by O'Neill and Corsi. Only one man out of Coastal Division 11 supported his bid. Most of the others actively campaigned against him.

Senator Kerry's campaign was a dichotomy; he touted his own service as heroic but condemned the war as unjust and immoral and his fellow servicemen as murderers and rapists. His quest for medals to boost his image was not satisfied by the US Navy but by the Communist North Vietnamese Government.

In the War Remnants Museum in Ho Chi Minh City (formerly Saigon) hangs a photograph of Kerry with the general secretary of the Communist Party of Vietnam, Comrade Do Muoi. The Communists appreciated Kerry's antiwar activism and still do.

Although Kerry lied about everything from being in Cambodia on Christmas to Al Hubbard's service as a pilot (not a pilot and not a Lt.Col.), he still managed to secure the Democratic Party's nomination in 2004.

The Swifties went into action without the boats and the .50 calibers. Armed with the book, "*Unfit for Command*," they sailed into political waters and sank John Francois Kerry. In a near landslide, George W. Bush was reelected for a second term.

In 2003, HR 1950, the Foreign Relations Authorization Act would have exposed the many atrocities committed by the Communist Vietnamese Government. Kerry took active steps to stop it as he had done two years earlier with HR 2833. Clearly he is an active advocate of the Communists.

In another day and time, under Lincoln, under Jefferson, under FDR, he would have been hanged. And despite the fraud, the lies and the Communist advocacy, he keeps getting reelected by a people who don't know or don't care what he does or what he is…a Communist, a traitor.

Jane Fonda should share a cell with him- ask any POW who met her in the Hanoi Hilton.

PCF Patrol Craft Fast

Comrade Kerry with his flag

Eighteen

Rules of Engagement

L imited or defense oriented warfare worked in Korea, but it was wrong for Vietnam. North Korea and North Vietnam both had the backing of the Chinese and the Soviets, but sentiment back home in the USA was different and became more so when the casualties and the cost mounted.

To announce sanctuaries for the enemy, keep hands off his main supply harbor and mark his capitol city off limits were egregious mistakes. The threat of an expanded war with China or the Soviet Union was real and should have been addressed early in the war. It was not. But if the decision was to risk it and go all out, the war would have ended differently, sooner and at a far less cost in blood and treasure.

The Quagmire of Vietnam was of our own making and history clearly has labeled it such. The rules of engagement made victory nearly impossible. Nearly... for General Giap recorded in his memoirs, "I did not understand why the Americans quit when they were so close to victory. They lost by a matter of days."

The numbers game in Vietnam was not the first time it had

been played. Hernan Cortes was told that he would have to kill 250 Aztecs for every man he lost. He didn't delay his attack or send to King Phillip for more conquistadors, he simply laid plans to kill 250 Aztecs for every man he lost, and Montezuma would oblige him.

At Khesanh, (Jan to April of 1968) where a bitter battle raged south of the DMZ, the enemy was losing fifty men for every American. The Communists didn't care. One NVA intelligence officer was quoted at saying, "His (Giap's) is not an army that sends coffins north; it is by the traffic of homebound American coffins that Giap measures his success."

Americans care about their fallen soldiers. But clearly the enemy had a manpower supply they were willing to sacrifice because they didn't care. A government controlled media in Hanoi did not tally every night the million plus war deaths suffered by the North. There was no LIFE Magazine to expose the lack of support given the NVA or complain that they were nearly out of SA-2 missiles, the air force down to a handful of MIG's.

On a local level, restrictions to safeguard the Michelin rubber plantation trees at Ben Cui prohibited artillery or air strikes by our forces. The enemy knew of the unofficial arrangement between our government and the French and took advantage it. Our men died.

The rules of engagement were stifling to our military. The comparisons of them to those in WWII are enumerated in "Carnage and Culture," by Victor Davis Hanson:

"No American army in 1944 would have fought the Germans in France without permission to cross the Rhine or bomb Berlin at will. Japan would have won WWII had the United States fought in the jungles and occupied towns of the Japanese empire, promising not to bomb Tokyo, mine harbors, attack its sanctuaries, or invade its native possessions, while journalists and critics visited Tokyo and broadcast to American troops from Japanese radio stations. Neither Truman nor Roosevelt would have offered to negotiate with Hitler or Stalin after

110

the successful Normandy landings or the devastating bombing campaign over Tokyo in March of 1945. GI's in WWII were killed in the pursuit of victory, not in order to avoid defeat or to pressure totalitarian governments to discuss an armistice. I n war it is insane not to employ the full extent of one's military power or to guarantee to the enemy that there are sanctuaries for retreat, targets off limits, and a willingness to cease operations anytime even the pretext of negotiations is offered."

OOO

So we fought a war with one hand tied behind our back with unwinnable rules of engagement and still almost won. When it was finally over President Richard Nixon would say, "It was after all, an honorable undertaking."

The American left reveled in their moment of triumph over our military. It was and still is the defining moment for Liberals. The problem is they turned away and hid their eyes to the carnage that followed in Southeast Asia. Which was exactly what we were trying to prevent and what was predicted by Dr. Tom Dooley in his speech tour in 1959. *"-They took chop sticks and jammed them into the ears of those nurses, making them deaf forever. Another group of nurses they herded into an ambulance and doused it with gasoline..."*

Deliver us from evil.

Nineteen

Give Me A Gun

T he F-4C Phantom is an awesome thing. Boasting two J-79 engines with after burners, she had 34,000 lbs. of thrust, capable of breaking the sound barrier in a vertical climb. It took two pilots to make it go. So versatile was this machine that all three services who have fighter planes adopted it for use.

With forward looking radar, it sported an array of heat seeking and radar controlled missiles; it had everything, everything but a gun. Designed to defend the fleet from incoming Soviet bombers, it didn't have a gun. Although many warnings from jet jocks across the squadrons were filed, none resounded with the Pentagon.

Growing dissatisfaction with the performance of the Sidewinder and Sparrow missiles fueled the debate again. Lt. Randy "Duke" Cunningham, USN, claimed he could have shot down seven or eight more MIG's if he had a gun on his F-4. The missiles flew erratically away from radar locked targets, were distracted by ground clutter or the sun or simply failed to fire. Others gave testimony to the Pentagon with equally chilling stories.

The Air Force reacted first. Their solution was a .20mm Vulcan cannon mounted in an exterior pod. On 6 November, '67, Captain Darrell D. Simmonds tangled with two MIG-17's within days of getting his gun. While the missiles were unsuited for the proximity of the engagements, the gun was not. He shot them both down in a three minute battle. He had trained for eight years for those three minutes, risking his life several times, but never again fired at the enemy, guns or missiles.

Eventually the F-4E model Phantom got an inboard gun and the pilots were happy. The new F-15, F-16, F-18 and Advanced Tactical Fighter all have cannons. The Phantom suffered Pentagonitis and had to endure in the most difficult of times when MIG's came out of cloud cover or snuck up from ground level behind decoys.

M-61 Vulcan 20mm cannon
Bbbrrrrrrrrpp!

TWENTY

IT

The old WWII fighter pilot smirked as he gazed into the camera, "If ya got it; ya can't teach it. If ya don't have it; ya can't learn it." He was talking about that intangible thing some call "fearless in battle," "cool under fire," or sometimes just "It."

The trouble with "It" is that you can't tell if you have it until you are in combat and in mortal danger. It matters not if you are in the air, on the ground, on the water or under the water.

George Custer had it. Eddie Rickenbacker had it. Audie Murphy had it, and John Basilone had it. Each would admit they were scared of failing more than of dying, and each was scared but put fear out of their consciousness.

The intangible quality is not limited to one race or one religious belief. In our nation's history we have awarded Medals of Honor to Whites, Blacks, Hispanics, Orientals, and Native Americans. Although George Custer did not receive the Medal of Honor his brother received two. 246 Medals of Honor were awarded during the Vietnam War.

Everyone who has "It" doesn't always receive a Medal of Honor, Navy Cross or Legion of Merit, but for those who did it's a good indicator. 180 Air Force Crosses and 491 Navy Crosses were awarded. There was no shortage of courage in our military forces in Vietnam despite arguments presented by the anti-war coalition.

They would point to the exception rather than the rule, the widespread use of drugs and always point to My Lai as if it were the defining moment of our involvement in Vietnam. The drug use was no more prevalent than with the population of non-military men at home. They would bring up the thousands of collateral damage casualties caused by our bombing and artillery, but in fact it was far less than in WWII where entire cities were flattened.

The conduct of our POW's was exemplary. Two Medals of Honor were awarded for resistance to the captors in prison rather than for valor in combat. And when North Vietnam was unwilling to repatriate our POW's, other men flew the B-52's to persuade them.

Those who burned their draft cards and fled to Canada were better off there. No one in Vietnam cared to share a foxhole with them. Obviously, they didn't have "It."

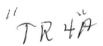

A Matter of Honor
By Daniel Rapp

It matters not what others see,
A peasant crude or polished lord
Or shining knight so gallantly
Slays the dragons with his sword.
What matters is inside of me
A place where Honor wants to be.

And if I fail in others' eyes
To do the things that they expect
The mirror will detect their lies
And haunt me in my self respect
But if I do what I think right
Honor backs me in the fight.

TWENTY-ONE

THE CHAPLAINS

They weren't supposed to fight and they weren't supposed to die, but thirteen chaplains were killed in Vietnam. Three would receive the Congressional Medal of Honor. Unlike the soldiers, most of them didn't know what unit they'd be assigned to until they were in-country.

The Congressional Medal of Honor was awarded to Charles Liteky for saving twenty wounded soldiers near Phuac Lac. Later as a peace activist he would renounce the medal and oppose the Iraq War. He demonstrated in Washington, not from Sadam's Headquarters, not on Al Jazeera.

Francis L. Sampson personified the chaplain's position in WWII, Korea and Vietnam. The Notre Dame ('37) graduate rose to be the chief of chaplains and retired a major general after thirty years.

- *"How can we send men into war without sending with them the ministers of God's word?"*

- *"Everyone thought I was being so courageous. They couldn't hear my knees knocking."*

- *"Someone asked if I would serve with the airborne. I said yes, and then I found out they expected you to jump out of airplanes with the men. I was too embarrassed to change."*

I see nothing in this mission that does not appear to the highest ideals of any man- regardless of his religion. Indeed, it was Cardinal O'Hara, the great Churchman who once said if he had not been a priest he would most certainly be a soldier, because they are both called to the identical things- that is- the preservation of peace, the establishment of justice when it has been lost, and the providing of security with protection of the weak and the innocent.
- Francis L. Sampson, chaplain, Major General.

Maj. Gen. Francis L. Sampson
(1912-1996)
Notre Dame 1937

Rev. Joseph F. O'Donnell, CSC, served from August, 1968 until January, 1970 aboard the USS Tripoli (LPH-10). In the field, in helicopters and aboard ship he was in and out of danger. He carried no weapons, only a paten and holy chrism for anointing the dying. His experience is chronicled in the book entitled *The Sword of the Lord; the History of Military Chaplains edited by Doris L. Bergen, Notre Dame Press 2005.*

Like many veterans he was not given a warm reception upon his return from Vietnam. Even members of his own religious community treated him with unspoken contempt, as if to say, "How could you support such an evil war?"

"—Support an evil war?" The only thing Tom Dooley found evil there was the enemy whose daily atrocities were given a bye from the media. Father Joe O'Donnell went to Vietnam to minister to the spiritual needs of Marines and sailors, not to kill the enemy's soldiers no matter how atrocious.

The perception of an evil war is a pacifist conclusion. "If nobody is willing to stand up to the communists in Southeast Asia the Domino Theory would be advanced," claimed the opposition. When the Dominoes fell in Vietnam those in Cambodia and Laos were not far behind. Father Joe O'Donnell's opinion never changed, "I did what was right! And I'm proud of my service to God and country."

He retired as a captain (O-6) in September of 1994 with nearly thirty years service.

Chaplain Joe O'Donnell rides the ship-to-shore helicopter

Joseph F. O'Donnell, CSC
Notre Dame '55

**Solemn moment for chaplain and Marines -
Field Memorial Service for thirteen Marines KIA**

TWENTY-TWO

THE HOME FRONT

A long protracted war with dubious rules of engagement began to wear thin on the American home front by 1969. After four years of it Secretary of Defense Robert McNamara would admit that the war was not winnable. Years after the war, in a meeting with North Vietnamese General Giap, he would finally admit it openly.

While a liberal press searched for shaky reasons to quit, college campuses erupted with demonstrations. The evening TV news brought yesterday's battle field to our living rooms. One family saw their son killed on TV because the network identified the unit and the man as a radio operator. The telegram and the chaplain arrived the day after.

An NBC affiliate in Atlanta, GA called Bob Hiscock to see a video which had just aired on the network. In the downtown studio he and his wife saw their only son talking about search and rescue operations for a fellow helicopter pilot shot down the day before. Twenty-four hours later they were told Skip was killed while searching for his friend.

When a VC mortar round set off the ammo dump at Dong Tam it appeared on TV as Armageddon. Fire and brimstone illuminated the night and relatives at home feared the worst for their loved ones stationed there. Fortunately casualties were mush less than expected.

POW families often weren't told if their son or husband was a prisoner or dead because the enemy would not disclose the names. Listed as MIA- missing in action, some weren't disclosed until 1973, only months before repatriation.

A battle death decimated an extended family, injecting grief into the memories of bye-gone family reunions, weddings and birthdays. The Fox family of North Tonawanda, NY, experienced the loss, the pain and the everlasting emptiness in November of '65. Son, Thomas J. of the First Infantry Division, had been in-country for 27 days when he was killed by mortar fire in Binh Duong Province.

Sixteen months later, the Bobo family of Niagara Falls, NY had to suffer the same. Their son, 2nd Lt John P. Bobo, USMC, was killed in Quang Tri Province. The pain suffered by his family was immeasurable. His memory lives on with a park and an American Legion Post named after him, but so does the emptiness of his loss. Posthumously awarded the Congressional Medal of Honor, John Bobo won't be forgotten.

Two heroes raised less than five miles apart probably never met in this life, but surely will in the next. Bound by the fellowship of righteous warriors, they'll have a lot to talk about.

By war's end 58,000 Americans had been killed, more than 2.5 million had served and at one point in 1969, 543,000 were in Vietnam at the same time. It was a war like no other we had ever fought. Only twenty percent fought in combat and eighty percent were support troops.

Our 766 POW's did not all return home safely; 114 died in captivity. 1719 are still listed as missing.

At home nothing was rationed. No shortages of gasoline, sugar, butter or rubber tires occurred like in WWII. The Government didn't sell war bonds and inflation was not particularly high. What made this war intolerable was its duration, ten years and an undetermined number of future fatalities. On 15 October, 1969 the Moratorium to End the War got wide spread support. A month later a massive Moratorium March on Washington was orchestrated.

We could bomb Milosevic's Serbians without a declaration of war by Congress as long as nobody was killed. But *freedom has a taste and price the protected never know,* whether it's our freedom or millions in Southeast Asia.

Rather than passing a law to stop the war, Congress simply withdrew funding. The bombs stopped falling, our POW's came home and the war ended with Russian built tanks crashing through the gates of the presidential palace in Saigon. It was April 30, 1975.

Pfc. Thomas J. Fox
(1944-1965)

2nd Lt. John P. Bobo (1943-1967)
USMC India Co. 3/9
Niagara University

USS 2nd Lt John P. Bobo (T-AK3008)

CWO-2 Stephen M. Hiscock
(1950-1971)

The Bugle Whispers Low
By Daniel Rapp

For those who man the battle line, the bugle whispers low,
And freedom has a taste and price the protected never know.
So tip your hat, say hello to someone who has served.
Raise your arm and hand salute the man who has been tried.
Raise your glass; toast *'hear-hear'* to those who never swerved,
Their mettle still unshaken when the sound of battle cried.

Know ye those whose blood has spilled in battle's bloody test,
Those who wear the *Purple Heart*, the medal on their chest
For through the haze of time and pain, they cannot forget
The men who fought beside them so many years ago.
The ones that did not come home again, fill their heart's regret.
The taste is bitter, my dear friend, the price is never low.

Whisper, whisper, you sound of bugle's note
Echo from the nearby hill, stick in valor's throat.
No end will come to honor's roll while we have men like these
Freedom's ring will echo too an everlasting song,
Played not on harp or flute but written on the breeze
By men who man the battle line and try to right the wrong.

TWENTY-THREE

PTSD

Post traumatic stress disorder (PTSD) is a type of anxiety disorder that's triggered by a traumatic event. You can develop PTSD when you experience or witness an event that causes intense fear, helplessness or horror. - Mayo Clinic staff

I n WWI they called it *shell shock*: in WWII they called *battle fatigue*. In Vietnam they called it *post traumatic stress disorder* (PTSD). No matter which war the mental effect on the minds of our service men is a scar often unseen until it flares with deep depression or violent rage.

In WWII our soldiers fought on average one battle every six months. In Korea it was four to six months. In Vietnam it was every three weeks. Remembering that a large number of troops were in support roles not combat roles, it is still difficult to comprehend why such a larger percentage of men suffered this disorder in Vietnam than in previous wars.

Recent research indicates that prolonged exposure to stress actually changes the chemistry of the brain. So it is possible that PTSD can be a physical as well as a mental disease. Most tours of Vietnam were limited to a one year period and men could look forward to the anniversary date. In the other wars they were in for the duration, often with no end in sight.

Self medication with everything from aspirin to alcohol to barbiturates may ease the effect of it and a busy mind can keep the demon at bay for years. Many found that while they worked a job, they had fewer flash backs or night mares. When they retired the mind was more receptive to the bad things they had stuffed into the attics of their minds.

The media often exaggerated the number of affected Vietnam veterans who suffered from PTSD and did so again in the Gulf War. Because they did does not mean there is not a problem still brewing. The Veterans Administration first denied the problem or at least ownership and then reversed itself to reach out to veterans and their families just as they had done with Agent Orange.

Military men are not the only ones affected by PTSD. Many civilians suffer it from attacks threatening life or sexual well being.

A wide range of symptoms follow the illness, flash-backs, sleep disorders, headaches, dizziness, feelings of isolation, and outbreaks of anger to name a few.

Healing wounded minds is as much our responsibility as healing wounded bodies.

Vietnam vets had all of the old illnesses of war and some new ones too, and they brought them home with them. More than 9,000 vets suffering from PTSD died by suicide.

TWENTY-FOUR

THROW A NICKEL ON THE GRASS

Hallelujah! Hallelujah!
Throw a nickel on the grass,
Save a fighter pilot's ass.
Hallelujah! Hallelujah!
Throw a nickel on the grass,
And you'll be saved.

Fighter pilots still sing the old refrain from the Korean War days. Oscar Brand made an album of it with some others such as "I Wanted Wings (until I got the goddam things)." They might still sing that one too.

Fighter pilots have historically been accused of being arrogant, boastful and self indulgent. How many NFL quarterbacks don't also have those same attributes?

With fighter pilots the win loss record takes on more than a Super Bowl or a shot at the Hall of Fame in Canton, Ohio. It's a life or death situations which often occur before the threat of combat with the enemy.

Performing an emergency procedure correctly, avoiding collisions with squadron mates and sometimes simply knowing the altitude of the surrounding terrain can be that crucial difference.

Thousands of would-be fighter pilots were killed learning their trade. The faster more complex became the aircraft, the greater the risk. In WWII pilots died because their radio chords wrapped around the landing gear crank. Others were killed because they ran out of fuel, misread the weather or failed to reset the barometric pressure on the altimeter.

The jet age F-86 Saber had a bad flying record until the pilots acclimated to the greater speed and different handling characteristics. With all the risks there has never been a shortage of young men willing to take them on for the thrill of horsing a silver bird around the sky. In Vietnam the numbers became staggering. They weren't there for the duration, usually 100 missions was enough to rotate back home or to the Philippines. Often they returned for a second tour of 100.

For all the negative images of fighter pilots, no one could deny their courage and dedication to duty. 1600 went "missing in action," over a hundred died in North Vietnamese prisons and over six hundred would endure the rigors of them.

One would land his heavy A-6 Skyraider in a field to save a fellow pilot, bullets striking the fuselage as he did. Many times pilots incurred great risk to themselves in the search and rescue efforts of downed flyers. Many augered in trying to provide infantry units close air support. They didn't crash, they augered in.

In the early years of the war tactics put fighter bombers into holding patterns over the target areas inviting radar directed Mig's to strike from out of cloud cover. Did the pilots complain? You bet! Did it do any good? NO.

As the war escalated Hanoi became the heaviest defended area in history, more than 5,000 guns and 25 missile battalions. More guns were positioned in the north than beleaguered

London or Stalingrad. SA-2 missiles were fired sometimes five at a time at one aircraft, and still our pilots kept flying north.

Only one Air Force fighter pilot would be an ace in Vietnam. Capt. Steve Ritchie shot down five Mig's in his Phantom fighter. The native of Reidsville, NC, a 1964 graduate of the Air Force Academy, earned four silver stars, ten distinguished flying crosses and the title of *ACE.* He didn't even have a gun.

Lt. Randall Cunningham was the only Navy pilot to become an ace in Vietnam. His record as an airman and an officer was overshadowed by corruption as a Congressman from California.

Old WWII pilots, still stuffed with the *right stuff,* taught and led the young guys in Vietnam. Robin Olds, Robinson Risner, Richard Mischke and Archie Donahue flew in wars more than twenty years apart. Risner spent six years as a POW.

Frederick "Boots" Blesse served in Korea and Vietnam, flying 154 combat missions in Laos and Vietnam. Boots was instrumental in establishing fighter tactics.

While envoys talked or failed to talk in Paris, the pilots flew north and the bombs fell until the enemy agreed to free the POW's.

Capt. Steve Ritchie
US Air Force Academy 1964

Col. Robin Olds USAF

Col. J. Robinson Risner USAF

Maj. Gen. Frederick "Boots" Blesse

Twenty-Five

Bookie Bird

Being a fighter pilot is dangerous but few people consider the dangers of flying a C-123 Provider in a backward country during wartime. Lt. Col. Paul J. Reinman USAF Ret. chronicles a year's tour in Vietnam where his squadron lost three aircraft and their crews. This is his story.

In February of 1970, while finishing my master's degree at the Air Force Institute of Technology (AFIT), I received my orders for Vietnam. I was to first attend a training school for the UC-123 defoliating aircraft and then report to Phan Rang AB, RVN. I thought at the time I must be one of the last Air Force pilots to go but found out later that many never did.

In early July I received amended orders. The Agent Orange operation, Project Ranch Hand, was winding down. This was lucky for me so I was never exposed to that material.

The new orders sent me to Lockbourne AFB for orientation to the C-123 Provider, often called the Bookie Bird. Powered by two radial reciprocating engines and two jet engines, it could takeoff and land on relatively short runways. I would soon find out how short.

John Kopf a classmate at AFIT was in my C-123 class and was also destined for Nam. Better still, we wound up on the same instructional crew. For six weeks we commuted between Dayton and Lockbourne, leaving Dayton each morning at 0530.

Our instructor had recent experience in Nam and he knew what he was talking about. Armed with his experience we trained for short field landings with steep approaches, air dropping, loose formations and lots of low altitude visual navigation over southeastern Ohio. We called it bush flying. Two of our classmates would later become generals, Frank Willis and Martin Ryan.

After 64 hours and 115 landings, we passed our tactical checks and were ready for the war. I returned to Dayton for a week's leave before departing.

25 September saw me waving goodbye to my wife and kids. A stop over in San Francisco allowed me to renew an old friendship with Pete Walmsley, my roommate from pilot training. Pete had flown L-19 air controllers in Nam but had converted to civilian life as a United Airline pilot. We cruised Lombard St. in his '65 Mustang; hit the Fisherman's Wharf and the Paul Masson winery.

On the evening of the 26th I boarded the Transcaribbean Airways stretch DC-8 with one B-4 bag, an A-3 parachute bag plus an attaché case. The DC-8 was outfitted for "maximum profit, minimum comfort." Our knees pressed into the seat in front. We sat in place through refueling at Hawaii and Guam, and finally were allowed to deplane at Clark AB in the Philippines.

No government quarters were available for the layover, so I stayed in a motel just outside the main gate. I was enjoying the night and the balmy weather when I noticed the ivy on the walls was alive with critters. 6" lizards common to Southeast Asia were everywhere, indoors and out. Although harmless, they made a weird sound like a   rattlesnake. In the next year I would see a lot of their cousins, some in frying pans.

The next week I attended jungle survival school, commonly called *snake school*.It was a gentleman's school compared to the real survival school I had attended five years earlier in Nevada. The gist of the course was to learn about the jungle and what to eat and what not to eat. It included how to get water out of vines and how to avoid capture. How to vector a rescue helicopter and use of the lift basket were also important.

The final exam was a night in the jungles just far enough away from anybody else so you had that *all alone feeling*. Slung in a hammock, I soon found out that the night sounds of the jungle were very similar to the north woods. Occasionally a roar or screech punctuated the night- Leopard, monkey?

Now and again a rat scurried across the hammock or rustled the leaves below. Needless to say, I did not sleep well.

The next morning was the escape and evasion exercise. We were tracked by Negrito natives, characters placed somewhere between Cro-Magnon and Homo-erectus in my National Geographic.

We were given two tokens to buy our freedom if they caught us. They turned the blood chit token in for the princely sum of a bag of rice. In the first exercise I picked a tangled mess of vegetation with a lot of insects. In thirty minutes one of the Negritoes found me. I paid him a token and headed for another hiding place. This one wasn't going to be so buggy. I sat down against a tree trunk and tried not to move. For two hours I was alone and then a Negrito came into view. He was looking intently away and then right at me. I didn't move. Although his body was mostly obscured by vegetation, I could see his entire face. I still didn't move. He made no motion towards me. In a minute he was gone.

I learned a valuable lesson. *Stay put even if you think you have been discovered*.

6 October, I departed Clark AB for Cam Rahn Bay. It was my first ride in a C-141 and I was a little apprehensive due to the steep pitch attitude on climb. A KC-135 tanker which I flew for

years would have stalled at that angle.

Cam Rahn Bay was a major seaport and a huge airport complex with dual 10,000 ft. runways and acres of pierced steel planking (PSP) ramp space. The passenger terminal was a huge open warehouse filled with all sorts of humanity, GI's, Vietnamese soldiers, their wives, their children, their dogs and chickens. Sleeping, eating, walking, running, the crowd was orderly mayhem.

Luckily the new vice-commander of the 35th Tactical Fighter Wing at Phan Rang was in my snake school and he had use of a C-47. He asked me if I wanted a lift instead of wading through the mess at the terminal. I naturally accepted. The C-47 made its way through the air without its main cargo door which had been removed. Things were different in-country.

We were greeted by the base commander at Phan Rang. Since we had circumvented the official in-country check in at Cam Rahn, we still had green backs in our possession and they were illegal tender. In-country everything was bought and paid for in military scrip or funny money. This was to prevent black market operations and hoarding. I borrowed five bucks from the base commander so I could have lunch.

When I checked in at Wing headquarters I was informed I was assigned to the 311th Airlift Squadron at Da Nang. The tail designation for the squadron was WV- willie vomit on the radio. Things were different.

So I went back to Cam Rahn in a C-123 and then on to Da Nang in a C-130. As the C-130 climbed out I could see the deep blue water, white sandy beaches, a dark green jungle, a perfect place for a resort if not for the war.

Da Nang was an old French base and it had old buildings and rusty barbed wire, a contrast to the new base at Cam Rahn. But it had aircraft, lots of 'em, OV-10's, C-130's, C-123's, CH-54 helicopters and a wing of F-4 Phantoms called the Gunfighters. A strange name it was considering they had only missiles and no guns.

142

I checked in with my detachment of the 311th and soon had my first exposure to death in the war zone. An aircrew had brought in the remains of several Korean soldiers from one of the outlying airfields. They had been buried for several days before they were found. Unfortunately one of the green body bags was torn and death's fluid leaked out onto the aircraft and onto the load master's flight suit. The odor was indescribably sickening. I never experienced so vile a smell again.

From the Ops building I was taken around the end of the runways to the other side of the field where our quarters were located. En route we passed the military mortuary. Part of our mission was to transport remains of men killed in action (KIA's) to Da Nang where the mortuary folks filled those aluminum caskets stacked in front of the building and sent them home. I passed that building every day on the way to work, a grim reminder.

My new home had been a storage room until I moved out some junk and some old furniture. I was left with a bed, a desk and a chest of drawers. With some scrounging I acquired some white paint and spruced it up a bit.

That evening I went to the *DOOM Club* (Da Nang Officers' Open Mess) for supper. It was pitiful; a far cry from the club John Wayne visited in the movie "The Green Berets."

Later that evening I understood why I was issued a helmet and a flack vest. A siren woke me from a light sleep. Several explosions followed. With helmet on, vest on and curled up under the bed I thought about my first day at work, the Korean bodies, the odor from hell, the stack of aluminum caskets and now rockets exploding in the neighborhood.

The next day I found that the rockets had damaged some aircraft, but nobody was injured. A tour introduced me to the BX, admin building, chapel and other facilities including a Vietnamese run massage parlor known to the locals as the *Steam & Cream*.

I was anxious to get started with my in-country checkout, but it had to be put on hold for a few days. A typhoon was approaching and the aircraft had to be evacuated to Phan Rang. Experienced crew members were needed, so I was left behind and went from *new guy* to detachment commander in a few days.

As the typhoon approached, maintenance troops asked to be issued M-16 rifles because of a "heightened threat" of Viet Cong attack. I resisted, thinking that they were more likely to shoot one another than be shot by the VC. In the end I was probably right in that no one was injured.

Once the typhoon passed we began flying operations once more, Qui Nhon, Peiku, Kontum, Phu Cat, Minh Long and Tien Phuoc. Some of these were 2000ft. strips off the beaten path. One day in late October as we descended beneath the clouds at 2000 ft. going into Quang Ngai two rounds of small arms stuff hit the rear of the aircraft. We climbed back into the cloud cover and headed for Da Nang. I wondered if they were VC shots or if some GI had slipped off the jungle trail to sanity.

By the end of October we had experienced engine failures, leaking windows and doors, low ceilings and the unavoidable monsoons. One day I flew all day and never got above 100 ft. Helicopters flew the beach and we flew a few hundred yards off shore.

Artillery takes high arcing paths to its target. Sometimes we got arty warnings and then radio silence. It was heart warming to again make contact with a fire base and have them tell us, "You should be out of the arty area in about ten miles." That would be about three or four minutes of deodorant failure.

Too often we flew missions to bring KIA's back to Da Nang. Duc Pho seemed to have more than their share of them. One evening we carried nine KIA's which filled the entire cargo bay with three rows of three. It was tough to imagine how those nine families would be affected.

Flying native civilians was not fun, especially in rough weather where one vomiter would set off a chain reaction. The tidal puke would roll forward in the cargo bay when we went nose down for landing. The crew in the cargo space would put on oxygen masks; we'd just open the side windows in the cockpit. Maj. Al Montecino, one of our pilots, hit a cow going into Tien Phuoc. No- the cow was on the ground. Stories surfaced about *blivots* bouncing along the ground but they were really egg shaped fuel tanks being off loaded while taxiing- *combat offload* we call it. They were pushed out the rear cargo door.

Nam had its lighter moments, most of them centered on our officers' club, the DOOM Club. Thanksgiving Day came and was almost gone when Al Montecino arrived from a full day of flying. Hoping he could at least get some leftovers, he ordered a turkey sandwich. The waitress returned with a glass and set it in front of him. "Turkey-seven," she stated. What Al was served was a Wild Turkey with 7-UP. He drank it and ordered a Doomburger.

The Doom Club offered megawatt bands on a weekly basis. Having a pair of ear plugs was mandatory. The Filipino and Korean versions of *The Doors* or *Led Zepplin* blasted the patrons of the Doom with such favorites as "Rorring Down the River," and the all time favorite, "We Gotta Get Outta This Place."

I finally got my aircraft commander check out on 20 November in Phan Rang and could fly solo. Soon after that, I flew a mission to Pleiku to pick up Vietnamese KIA, his wife and child. I can still picture the casket draped with the red and yellow Vietnamese flag illuminated by the lights of the fork lift. The rest of the space around the casket was cast in darkness. The war was never very far away.

On 29 November I learned that my friend Norbert (Britt) Podhajsky was killed in the crash of a C-123 between Phan Rang and Cam Rahn Bay. Finding the wreckage in the jungles took nearly a week. Several F-100 pilots died with him as they headed for their "freedom bird" that would have taken them home. Britt is the only one that I knew whose name is on the

Vietnam Wall in Washington.

Having been transferred from Da Nang to Phan Rang my duties changed to duty controller, assisting and keeping track of flight crews. We were provided guidance from the Airlift Control Center in Saigon (known as *Mother*) and given local information from the Airlift Control Elements located at most of the major airfields. When I arrived the mood was gloomy having lost two aircraft in a short period.

My new job was clear cut, twelve hour shift, six days a week. An NCO assistant was assigned to the shift with me. We started at 0400 when we received the fragmentary orders from *Mother*. Sometimes boring and sometimes hectic when the problems with maintenance and weather intervened, but the job was always interesting.

By 1600 the aircraft started returning and some we had lost radio contact got worrisome, but they always returned. Some made it in with the sun all but gone on the horizon and the sky glowing like a luminous ceiling.

My flying duties had lessened with the new job but I got some flights scheduled during free time. At other off times I tried to solve recurring problems, like strong cross winds. They tended to roll the C-123 over because of the narrow dimension between the left and right landing gear. We tied a tug or APU to weight the wing down and the tug drove alongside while the aircraft was taxiing. A bit cumbersome it was.

A passenger flight in a C-123 is not like in an airliner. There is a urinal but no toilet. Stacked up in traffic at Bien Hoa and waiting to take off, a passenger had a shit attack. I told him to hold it until we got to Cam Rahn Bay, twenty minutes after take off.

Once in the air the crew chief called on the intercom to tell me the passenger crapped in the garbage can. I told the crew chief to advise him of the old Air Force rule, "Whoever uses the aircraft latrine first has to empty it."

After we landed I saw a guy dragging the garbage can across

the ramp to empty it. When ya gotta go...

By mid December Christmas started popping up. One C-7 Caribou had its nose painted like Santa. They called it Santa Bu. I remember attending midnight Mass on Christmas and walking back to my quarters under an absolutely clear sky with stars as far as you could see (Polaris almost on the northern horizon) and perhaps 80 degrees F. It was hard to imagine what Christmas was like at home when it was so different here, different in so many ways.

Once Christmas was over I settled back into the old routine of command post duty and occasional flying, typically 6 days or so a month. Being shot at was still a possibility but the more proximate dangers lie in the weather and the terrain. While flying the coast line I made the turn towards a bay which led to the airfield further inland. I had just completed the 90 degree turn when I saw through the haze that I had turned into the wrong bay. I was headed into a box canyon with no exits. The passengers and crew didn't get any heads up warning; a violent right turn took us out of the bay and back on course to the correct bay. After that rude awakening, I watched the landmarks more closely. This was bush flying and the landmarks figured heavily in most of the navigating.

Rest and recuperation (R&R) was allowed that wasn't charged to leave time. I made use of this by meeting Nancy in Hawaii for a week. The Waiohai Resort was fabulous, $16 per day for half of a beachfront cottage- the last of the good deals. By 22 June I was back at Phan Rang.

Operations were uneventful until mid-August when I briefed a crew for an insect control spraying mission over Phan Rang. A young lieutenant pilot, a lieutenant colonel navigator and a crew chief took off on schedule and flew their mission. About the time they should have returned I got a phone call from the tower, "Your aircraft is down."

I asked, "You mean it has landed?"

"No, it has crashed and there are probably no survivors,"

answered the tower. The tower called the crash crew and I called the wing commander and flying safety officer. Reports throughout the morning confirmed that there were no survivors. Only when my shift was over could I drive to the crash site. I realized quickly that the aircraft had struck the ground in an almost vertical attitude. The wreckage was confined to a 100 ft. radius.

The subsequent accident investigation board revealed that the pilot had made a high speed pass down the runway and then made a steep pull up. The aircraft lost power or simply stalled and plummeted straight into the ground

After that a pilot didn't know he had flown his last mission until it was over and the Ops officer greeted him after landing. He was then ceremoniously thrown into the shower, and finished his tour with ground duties.

Flying an aircraft to Taipei for "Inspection and Repair as Necessary "(IRAN) was an operational perk. When my turn came up we took off with a full load of fuel, a shopping list and lots of cash to buy lamps, room dividers, bars, books, cameras, etc.

While they worked on our aircraft, ol' WV591, we went shopping and enjoyed being tourists. The nose wheel of 591 was troublesome and mechanics at Phan Rang could never seem to get it right. After an eleven day wait, we were given another aircraft and returned to Phan Rang on 11 September. Our cargo weight (shopping binge) was unknown but the crew chief balanced it well and we had an uneventful return flight.

I was greeted by the Ops officer who told me I had just flown my last mission in Vietnam. I took the mid-day shower.

When I prepared to return home my baggage weighed 1,351 pounds and filled ten hand made plywood cases. Remember I started with a suitcase, a parachute bag and a brief case.

26 September I boarded my "freedom bird" for home. A spontaneous cheer went up from the passengers as soon as the wheels were in the wells.

It was a year that I will never forget. It was not something I care to repeat, but I think that I gained an appreciation for what I have. We went there for what appeared a noble cause, but somewhere along the way we lost our goal. Someone once said that for what the war cost us we should have bought the country and turned it into a resort with white sandy beaches, deep blue waters and dark green jungles. Let the Japanese manage it. Hopefully in the future, its full potential will be realized.

Military scrip

Lt. Col. Paul J. Reinman USAF
Newark College of Engineering '59

C-123 Provider

C-123 named "Patches" took 567 bullets and shell fragments in Vietnam. It resides at the National Museum of the Air Force in Dayton, Ohio.

Paul Reinman works as a volunteer restoration mechanic at the museum. Among other duties he polishes with TLC the C-123 aircraft "Patches."

Bob Stevens'

"There I was..."

WE DEDICATE THIS PAGE TO THAT RECENTLY RETIRED OLD WORKHORSE, THE C-123 "PROVIDER." PILOTS IN 'NAM CALLED HER THE "BOOKIE BIRD." SHE WAS NO BEAUTY QUEEN. BUILT FROM THE PLANS OF A DEFUNCT TOWED GLIDER, SHE DEPENDED ON TWO OL' R-2800 ROUND ENGINES TO BLAZE ALONG AT ABOUT 125 KTS!

DESIGNED FOR SHORT-FIELD OPERATIONS, SHE HAD SOME WEIRD INSTRUMENTATION-LIKE NO OIL QUANTITY GAUGES and SWITCHES THAT WOULD JETTISON ALL FUEL —

THE INTERIOR WAS, UH, SPARTAN —

Twenty-Six

Electronic Warfare

The B-52 was twenty-five years old when it began taking trips to Viet Nam. Col. Tofie Owen Jr. took thirty missions to the DMZ as an electronics warfare office and then several more in reconnaissance C121s. Armed with his experience, he went to the Pentagon to make electronics work better. This is his story.

Tour 1: Arc Light Missions

Arc Light was the code name given to the use of the B-52s in support of conventional bombing during the war. I was assigned to the 7th Bomb Wing, 9th Bomb Squadron, at Carswell AFB, Texas as an Electronic Warfare Officer (EWO) flying B-52Fs.. The role of the EWO is to alert the crew to enemy attack and to use self protection measures such as radar jammers, chaff, and flares to protect the aircraft against both ground based and air attacks.

The use of B-52s in Vietnam represented a radical change in their mission from one of strategic bombing with nuclear weapons to conventional bombing with iron bombs. We started preparation for this new mission in the early fall of 1964. It was not until the spring of 1965 that the orders came to deploy to Andersen AFB in Guam. Our mission was to hit Viet Cong targets in South Vietnam. Unfortunately, shifting from a strategic mission to a conventional mission presented a challenge. Previously a single aircraft operated alone. With the change in mission, you coordinated three waves of ten aircraft. Operating with a total of thirty aircraft in formation was vexing, especially when some of the old strategic tactics were still in place. On the very first mission two B-52s collided as they loitered awaiting the refueling tankers.

I deployed in July 1965 and returned home in November 1965. Our missions were about 13 hours long. I believe in that time frame I flew something on the order of 30 combat missions. Obviously in any war there are always a number of occurrences you never forget.

One such occasion was the night we were getting ready to take off on a mission with each aircraft in trail. Something happened on the aircraft in front of us as we were taxing for take off. The bombs loaded on both wings of that aircraft accidentally jettisoned due to some malfunction. There we were trying to get out of the way of several live bombs littering the taxiway, not something you would ever expect to happen.

Another interesting episode was the Saturday morning we were all awakened to do an unscheduled mission. Our task was to provide what was essentially close air support to a group of US Marines that were pinned down in the northern part of South Vietnam at Khe Sanh. I think we were all taken back by this tasking. No one had even imagined that a B-52 would be called in to do essentially close air support. The fear factor was high but not that we would be shot down. We were more afraid of hitting our own Marines. But thank heaven the mission was a success and our brave Marines were not hit. Flat plate antennae placed on their perimeter served as beacons and the bombs fell outside the perimeter with pinpoint accuracy. Sometimes thirty B-52s a day visited Khe Sanh. To the enemy it must have been terrifying.

When you are dropping as many bombs as a B-52 carried, you were always concerned about target placement and the accuracy of the bomb drops. I recall a surprise visit by the Commander in Chief of Strategic Air Command (CINCSAC). He attended the debriefing of the mission we had flown earlier that day. Unfortunately it was a day in which many of our bombs hit to the right of target and, to say the least, he was not a happy camper. At that point our provisional commander, MG Crum, stood up and pointed out on a map that to the left of the target was either a school or a hospital. He told the CINC that his men may have erred but they erred on the side of not hitting anywhere near that school or hospital and that is why so many of the bombs fell off target.

The B-52s were nicknamed the Black Knights of the Mekong. In preparation for the conventional mission, the bottom of the B-52s had to be repainted from the white surface to black so as not to be seen at night. When we redeployed back to Carswell AFB, we had a general officer visit us who was not enthralled with the idea of using B-52s in a conventional role and quickly pointed out that he wanted the aircraft repainted white. Never the less, other more senior Air Force officers saw the value and continued with the use of B-52s until the war ended

As the war progressed, B-52s were moved from Guam to Utapao in Thailand. It was soon realized that the B-52s could play an even more valuable role in the war, conducting strikes in North Vietnam. Thus the Line-Backer operations were possible which brought the North Vietnamese back to the table in Paris. Nixon's bombing campaign became a turning point for us. We repatriated our POW's and helped to bring an end to that horrible, drawn-out conflict.

Tour 2: Bat Cat Missions

My second wartime tour was in Korat Thailand, most famous

for the Wild Weasels. But my assignment was different. I was assigned to the 553rd Recon Wing from November 1968 to November 1969. Our mission was to detect troop or convoy movements using sensors that were on the ground. Our aircrafts were slick back EC-121s borrowed from the Navy out of the grave yard at Davis Monthan AFB. While my role was as an Instructor EWO, the actual mission crew was made up of about a dozen people. They were to listen to ground sensors and report any movements to the USAF. Needless to say the missions may have had questionable value. Under the approved Rules of Engagement (ROE), the sensor crew on the EC-121 was to relay the info back to a base in Thailand. Then they would call in the strikes. With the time lag many of the convoys had already moved on by the time the strikes occurred.

Our missions were long, generally around 13 or 14 hours with about twelve of those orbiting the area. For the most of the missions it was pretty quiet in terms of actual enemy attacks on our aircraft, but every once in a while they would try something different.

One night while orbiting, we could see a reflection of something bright as it just happened to be a full moon. The enemy had used an old World War II tactic called a barrage balloon. They had launched a derigble with trailing wires several thousand feet long. The objective was to snarl our props thereby causing us to crash. Fortunately, the bright moon enabled us to see what they were doing and we took evasive action.

One of the most emotional events occurred on a night mission. I had to make a radio announcement that I had detected a radar site associated with an anti-aircraft battery. When I did, someone on the radio responded "Is that you, Tofie?" It was a classmate of mine from grad school. He was on a strike mission and had come under attack. Not knowing exactly where he was, I immediately turned on our Electronic Warfare equipment but it was not clear what immediately followed. The next week I learned that he was shot down and was missing in action. It was long after the war that I found out that he had been killed. The war was not so big that two friends could meet in the darkened skies, if only for a moment.

My experiences at Korat were not just about the war but also about people. Our crew, which totaled 21 (the flight crew plus the mission crew), knew that it would be tough being away from our families during Christmas. So for Christmas Eve, we arranged to go to the local orphanage and spend the evening with the kids. It was one of the most emotional experiences of my life. I will never forget the smile of the little five year old girl as she sat on my lap. I helped her open her gifts. In a letter to my wife, Margaret, I told her that being there with those kids helped salve the sadness of being away from her and our own kids.

As in any year long tour during the war, many other episodes played out. Some were uplifting, others terribly sad. While we never lost an EC-121 to enemy attack, we did lose one to weather. For some unknown reason, the aircraft commander decided to launch from Korat with a major thunderstorm at the end of the runway. Unfortunately, the updraft and then the sudden down draft caused the aircraft to crash. All of the crew perished. Besides the terrible loss of life, it was to be the last mission for the pilot before he was to rotate home and retire. You just never know what goes thru one's mind in times like that.

As the months marched on during the year long tour, our crew had the opportunity to either go to Australia or Hawaii for R&R. However if you didn't select one of those two, then you had the option of taking a week's leave back in the states and then a week in Taipei, Taiwan. We chose the latter and both of those ended up with unforgettable experiences.

In June of 1969, I went home on leave to Gulfport, MS. On the way back I was fortunate enough to catch a hop on a tanker from Carswell back to Utapao. My plan was to hire a taxi to take me back to Korat along with another crewmember who was heading there too. Unfortunately, as we got out of the main area of Utapao, our taxi blew his engine. There we were. It was night time in a desolate, high-crime area of Thailand, on a road less traveled. Finally we were able to hitch a ride on a Thai truck carrying supplies from Utapao to Korat. The flat bed truck carried a tarp over some unknown and unseen cargo. Since four Thais already occupied the cabin, we were stuck riding on top. During the four hour drive we bounced all over the place. Between the bad driving, the rough roads and then finally a heavy tropical thunderstorm, we were miserable. The two of us decided to see if we could get some cover by getting under the tarp. When we lifted the tarp, we were amazed and petrified by what we discovered. We were sitting on LIVE BOMBS, 500 pounders. Fortunately, someone above was looking out for us and we made it back safely. What an experience!

Two months later, I was with my crew on R&R in Taipei. I had just gone back to my hotel from a shopping trip. As I lay down on the bed and turned on the radio to listen to the Armed Forces Network, I was startled by the announcement that followed. Words I will never forget, "We interrupt this program to bring you a special announcement. Downtown Gulfport Mississippi has been destroyed by Hurricane Camille." No words can express the apprehension that I felt. My entire family, wife, kids, parents, brother, sisters, aunts, uncles and cousins all lived in Gulfport.

I immediately tried to get a call thru the US Navy base to my home. That didn't pan out. I tried the US Embassy and they were no help. But the hotel desk clerk came to my aid and pointed out that the Taipei telephone exchange was just down the street and I should go talk with them. They got me through on a telephone call to my wife. She still had telephone service, but because of the loss of power, she had no idea how bad the storm was nor what toll that it had taken on our family and others on the Gulf Coast.

November rolled around and I had my new assignment, Warner Robins Air Logistics Center in Georgia.

Tour 3: Robins AFB

Assigned as Chief of the Avionics Engineering Management Section, I oversaw all of the logistics engineering for avionics. Much of it was in support of our war in Vietnam. I found myself engaged in major activities from the initial modification and deployment of the AC-130 Gunship to major updates to our operational EW (electronics warfare) equipment. So for the next four and a half years, the war was never far away. We stayed busy supporting the pressing requirements of the Vietnam Conflict.

All of these experiences prepared me to move on to the Air Staff in the Pentagon, eventually heading up Electronic Combat on the R&D staff It was from that position that I retired and moved on to civilian life. The war seemed so distant then, but some parts of it will never be forgotten

Beresford's Bruins & EC-121 (Owen front row center)

**B-52 cuts loose 750lb bombs on the Ho-Chi Minh trail.
(Notice the black painted underside of the aircraft)**

Col. Tofie Owen Jr.
(Notre Dame '59)

TWENTY-SEVEN

DICKEY CHAPELLE

The song by Nanci Griffith goes "She was born Georgette but the name didn't serve her well, so, she blew out of Wisconsin as Dickey Chapelle." Georgette Meyer Chapelle was one of a kind, a pilot, an engineering student at MIT, a war correspondent and a world famous photojournalist.

Born in Shorewood, Wisconsin, March 14, 1918, Dickey Chapelle went to war in the Pacific with the Marines on Iwo Jima and Okinawa. Again in Korea she braved the dangers of combat to tell with her camera what she couldn't tell with words.

Ironically, the most famous pictures were of her rather than by her. Although she won the National Press Picture of the Year Award in 1963, the most famous picture was of her death. This bigger than life adventurer loved the Marines, followed them into battle and eventually died with four of them on November 4, 1965 near Chu Lai, Republic of Vietnam.

She was the first woman journalist killed in the Vietnam War, victim of a trip wire mine. Her story is told in the book entitled "Fire in the Wind: The Biography of Dickey Chapelle," by Roberta Ostroff.

Dickey Chapelle in WWII U.S. correspondent uniform
[See Wisconsinhistory.org pg 5 copyright]

Chaplain John McNamara administers last
rites to mortally wounded Dickey Chapelle

DICKEY CHAPELLE

The Camera's Eye
By Daniel Rapp

Her camera went to war, behind it went her eye
Fearless in the face of it, she never questioned why.
'Not my job.' she answered those who questioned her resolve.
'The war is someone else's doing, not mine is it to solve.
I photograph Marines at war and show that they fight well.
No shrinking violet do you see, my name is Dickey Chapelle.'

On Iwo and Okinawa her eye was younger then.
And Korea had its moments but that was way back when.
'War has not changed so much, still bullet and bomb,
And now this awful thing we have in goddam Vietnam.
And so the camera tells the tale as only it can do.
My picture tells a thousand words just like I want it to.'

'I expect some day that fate will come creeping up on me.
I only hope I'm on patrol, it's where I oughta be-
Not filming some peace parade in Washington, DC
I'll take my lumps just like they, when fate calls out to me.'
And so she did once too often dip water from the well.
Then fate came knocking and harshly took Dickey M. Chapelle.

TWENTY-EIGHT
THE ENEMY

The communist system has two classes, the proletariat or ruling class and the bourgeoisie or peasants. Never were these two classes more clearly defined than in Vietnam, before, during and after the war. Nearly two million Vietnamese people died in their war of liberation, few of those were the proletariat.

After the war, North Vietnamese fighter pilots became cab drivers not airline pilots. Infantry officers took on menial jobs. Viet Cong guerrillas, who lived through it, went back to their meager homes. The ruling class remained the ruling class.

All the things promised- free elections, land reform, and personal rights, were never fulfilled. Today the country welcomes American tourists and tries to sell their textiles and machine tools here at home. The minimum wage is about $36 per month.

Antiquated utilities and an inferior infrastructure impede progress and foreign investment. In short, the system hasn't worked in thirty-five years. Although GDP has increased 5.3% in 2009, the rate isn't close to China or India.

In the ensuing years since the fall of Saigon, they have

become more like us, not we who have become more like they. Registered private industry contributes as much as 11% of GDP with only 7% of the jobs and contributes 25% of the industrial output of the country.

Since 1989 religious persecution by the government has lessened. Periodic pressure occurs on religions considered to be a threat. Buddhism, Confucianism and Christianity are practiced with some degree of tolerance.

A generation has grown old since 1975 and with it the veterans who stayed in Vietnam, their atrocities forgotten and never mentioned in the war museums where My Lai gets its own display case. The 6,000 murders in Hue and 31,000 others elsewhere are dismissed as unwanted bourgeoisie.

The North Vietnamese Air Force listed sixteen air aces compared to only two American aces of the war. It could be explained away easily that the North Vietnamese pilots had many more targets of opportunity and chose their time to fight, but the enemy pilots had ground radar directing them and were very resourceful in their attacks. Often they used decoy aircraft with trailing fighters at low altitude to cover them. Painted camouflage, these low-boys were hard to spot visually until improved radar in the Phantom F-4 series could detect them.

Ground based anti-aircraft guns and radar controlled Surface to Air Missiles (SAM's) grew in great numbers in the north and then in the DMZ until North Vietnam had the world's most intense anti-aircraft network.

All tolled, more than 1600 American fixed wing aircraft were lost to enemy action, while another five hundred were operational losses.

**Viet Cong woman apprehended with 15 grenades
Oct 1972, near Da Nang**

North Vietnamese Mig-21 pilots

**Soviet-built tank of the North Vietnamese Army
crashes the gates of the Presidential Palace in the
Fall of Saigon, April 30, 1975**

It has been well documented that Russian pilots saw action in Viet Nam and thus were more than advisors. The Chinese also contributed to the Communist war effort as advisors to the pilots, gunners and anti-aircraft missile battalions of North Viet Nam.

Without the financial aid and loans from China and the Soviet Union, Ho Chi Minh could not have sustained a ten year war. At its peak the air defenses around Hanoi were the most intense in the world, 150 radar stations, 150 SAM sites, 8,000 conventional anti-aircraft guns and 105 fighter interceptors. It took 110,000 people to man the massive air defense system.

North Vietnamese Gen. Vo Nguyen Giap

Jane Fonda with her North Viet Namese comrades.

TWENTY-NINE

IN THE HOT SEAT

From 1964 to 1974 2.1 million Americans served a wartime tour in South East Asia. Some served two tours and a few served three. John F. Conlon of Shortsville, NY was one of the few, serving three tours in three different capacities. Being there in the beginning, the middle and the end he was one of a select number who witnessed the three phases while sitting in the hot seat. This is his story.

When I arrived in country in 1964 the philosophy was to create a counter insurgency force of indigenous troops to battle the communist Viet Cong (VC). Being one of only twelve officers selected for the task we were on untested ground. We had no track record on the Viet Namese or Cambodian volunteers so we didn't know how well they would fight.

With the responsibility of recruiting a force of 2500 men we couldn't afford to be choosy. Two Cambodians joined for every Viet Namese. They came across the border for a pay scale that was ten or twelve times what they saw on the farms and miniscule factories where they had worked. While they were motivated by money, their Viet Cong adversaries were

173

motivated by ideology, at least for the most part. Some VC were young men or teenagers kidnapped by their superiors and forced to fight.

The camps were constructed with money from the CIA and the recruits were paid from the same checkbook. We trained these men as best we could with a three week boot-camp, equipping them with WWII vintage M-1 rifles. The rifles weren't in their hands all the time. We were afraid of accidental discharges and spies so the rifles were issued for a combat patrol or sentry duty and then taken back. The rifle weighed 13 lbs. and was simply too heavy for those small bodied men. Years later the light weight M-16 weapon was made operational but it was lost in the future at the time.

Speaking of spies, we always had the threat of men volunteering to join us but with the intent of spying or sabotaging our camp facilities. In hind sight, they probably did do just that but I was never positive. The worst thing I was positive about was my stolen boots. Put out to dry in the sun both pairs were stolen. There is not a single Viet Namese person in the world that could fit a 13B shoe. Who could wear them?

After summoning the commander of the irregulars I told him if I didn't have my boots back in an hour, their mess hall would be closed until further notice. I got my boots back. If that had not worked I was already planning on canceling payday at the end of the month.

My sector of camps was in the Mekong Delta in an area called the Southern Mountains, near the Cambodian border. They called us a para-military organization. I guess para-military means Not-quite military. Those guys must have had a silent motto, "Not too aggressive-- Live to fight another day." I felt, with this force of mercenaries, I was a little warlord in a strange far away land. I wore a green beret. I oughta write a book.

For all our short comings, the VC had a different set of problems: no medical support, long supply lines, unsecured base camps and an enemy that could pound them with heavy mortars all night long. And pound them we did. It was not unusual to expend 500-600 rounds of 81mm mortars and 105mm howitzer shells and have them replaced by morning. We had helicopters, they didn't. We had some air support, they had none.

The fledgling Viet Namese Air Force was not very effective, young pilots and old planes with small payloads. When GI pilots supported us they always wanted a damage assessment. In all honesty that was tough. We didn't want to send someone outside the wire to look and the VC always tried to carry off their dead and wounded. I would say "Wait a minute, I'll check." I'd hold the receiver against my chest for a couple minutes and then come back on, "You got six of them and a heavy machine gun." The pilots would let out a cheer over the radio, but truthfully, we rarely knew how effective they were. I had to make them feel they were contributing for I would surely need them again.

Small single engine observation planes flew over our camps and I personally saw three of these "Piper Cubs" shot down. To me it didn't seem like a good idea to get so close to small arms fire of the enemy; the heavy machine guns could be menacing.

Aggressive patrolling was a big factor in keeping the VC at bay. If you spend two-thirds of your effort patrolling outside the camp you have one-third left to protect the camp itself. I felt the imbalance was worthwhile. On one evening patrol we were on the edge of a canal that was swollen by an unusually high tide. The canal paralleled the Cambodian border and a road paralleled the other side of the canal. Our patrol included three jeep mounted machine guns. Just before dark I saw a bunch of black dots upstream. After taking cover, I realized the dots were VC paddling towards us in sampans, three or four men to a sampan.

We waited until the sampans were 500 yards away when we opened up with everything. We took minimal return fire and in a matter of minutes the enemy force was decimated. Our machine gun barrels were so hot we had to pour water on them before we could move them. Darkness had fallen so we could not access the damage until sunrise. At 07:00 we returned to find the tide had gone out leaving the canal banks littered with bodies and splintered sampans. I remember thinking, if we had left ten minutes earlier, we never would have seen them coming. We would have had a bad awakening around midnight.

As required by HQ we took a body count but there was no telling how many caught the outgoing tide and were then feeding the fish in the South China Sea. Total, I estimated at 70 plus VC were killed in the ambush. This time Charlie was on the short end of the stick. Sometimes you just had to out-Charlie Charlie.

When the VC were detected in the immediate neighborhood we would conduct H&I (Harass & Interdict) operations. At irregular intervals we'd lay down a barrage on the known trails leading to our camp. It kept them off balance; they never mounted a really big attack where we were in danger of being overrun. Other camps didn't fare as well.

My friend Roger H.C. Donlon's camp at Nam Dong was nearly overrun one morning in July. The radio traffic was intense and everyone thought it was Conlon in trouble not Donlon. A VC reinforced battalion, 800-900 strong, stormed his outer perimeter and main gate. Two of the twelve Green Berets were lost and several wounded. He was wounded several times himself. For his part in the camp's defense Donlon was the first Medal of Honor recipient of the war.

In hind sight I was fortunate that my combat experience came in small doses at first. I cannot over emphasize the importance of combat experience. Everything is so much more manageable, you aren't rattled by the complexities of battle or thinking about failure or even about getting killed. You do your job and you and your men are the better for it. Calling in artillery or air strikes, reacting with reserve troops to pressure points, coordinating ammo resupply- all those things have to be handled in orderly fashion without your voice going up two octaves or your hands trembling.

The camps were under constant pressure and when I rotated back home I felt I was lucky to be alive. Now someone with little or no experience had to take my place and that was a concern. The one year tour would haunt us for the rest of the war- those more likely to survive and lead effectively left the war to men less capable simply because they didn't have experience. The learning curve became even steeper as the war escalated and the People's Republic of Viet Nam sent more and more well trained and disciplined troops from the North.

OOO

In 1966 I returned to the war in a different capacity. The 1st Air Cavalry Division needed company commanders-- I volunteered. We had 488 helicopters including gunships. Air power had evolved into a big part of the war effort. Directing air strikes was now a big deal and I had gotten good at it. The old T-28 and B-26 aircraft were replaced with Skyraiders, modern F-100 and the latest F-4 Phantoms. They carried huge bomb loads of 500lb. high explosive and the devastating napalm. My air strike directing skills improved with time and experience and yet the Army and the Air Force never had a school to teach me that important trade.

We had all kinds of support, even a battle ship. 16" guns firing from twenty-five miles away aren't very accurate. I usually had them fire a mile or so long but a couple times they came too close for our own comfort. The huge shells sounded like freight trains flying overhead-- scary. The enemy probably thought so too.

The Federal Government paid for a lot of unnecessary ordinance because of me! Yeah, if anything, I used too much -

better to err on the safe side. My command took casualties but I always felt they were less than comparable units put in similar situations. The difference was overwhelming air and artillery support and I wasn't afraid to use it.

The company commander who preceded me had a personal policy of sending thirty-day short timers back to relatively secure areas. He got them admin jobs or mess duty. By doing that he weakened his position by 8%. I didn't like it. I ordered the first sergeant to bring them back, all except the ten-day short timers.

A few days later, one of the short timers climbed a tall rock out cropping on the base perimeter. A VC sniper took advantage of his mistake and killed him on the spot. The decisions of command had its consequences, as if I hadn't already found that out.

I stuck to the ten-day short time rule though. The entire company was short handed and more vulnerable with the other policy. Everybody else faced more danger to lessen it for a few.

The 1st Cav was a reactionary force. We went to places where the trouble had already commenced. Hot landing zones were the norm rather than the exception. On one mission we could only get about 40 men into the landing zone when the helicopters came under such intense fire that they stopped coming in. We were informed that we couldn't expect ammo resupply and nightfall was closing in. We were up against a North Viet Namese regiment sized unit; our only trump card was the artillery located some ten or twelve miles away. Like I said, I wasn't afraid to use it.

Incoming small arms fire was heavy and I couldn't avoid all of it. A bullet passed through my left arm. Yeah, it hurt like hell but I had a job to do. While visiting the various positions on our perimeter I found a soldier on the verge of hysteria. "I've been wounded, Sir. Look." He showed me his wound. It was exactly like mine, through the left arm. "I need medical attention," he pleaded. I responded that medics didn't make it in before we were surrounded. "You'll have to tough it out, soldier."

It was about midnight when we spoke. I left him with some harsh words about covering his sector 15 degrees to the left and 30 degrees to the right and not letting anybody through. "I don't want to find somebody firing at my back. Do your job."

When first light came about six AM the enemy withdrew and I was able to make rounds again. The soldier with a wound like mine was dead, ashen white and cold. It must have been shock that killed him. Maybe I was too rough on him, I don't know. It still bothers me though.

When daylight illuminated my fatigue jacket I saw that both front pockets had bullet holes in them. My dog tag chain had been nipped while slack- that's close and the tags were loose in my undershirt at the belt line.

When I tried to give headquarters a disposition report they told me the artillery bases had fired 16,000 rounds. Some had fallen 100ft. from our own positions. We counted 450 dead enemy soldiers, most of them in pieces. No telling how many they carried off. The artillery had held them off all night and we had no barbed wire or concertina strung to keep them out, just firepower.

For my wound I received the Purple Heart. For directing the artillery and conducting our defensive perimeter I received the Silver Star. Amazingly it was only the third Silver Star awarded the 1st Cav in eighteen months of combat. The politics of the war had turned ugly and citations were being down played, even discouraged. Some good men deserved awards that they never got, never even got recommended.

In late December of '66 my command was down to eighty-five men because of rotation, sick and wounded. At nightfall one hundred new recruits were dropped on me to fill the ranks. A big air assault operation was set for daybreak. Most of the new men didn't know how such an operation went down. We tried to brief them in the short time available.

"First off, the artillery will bombard the landing zone for

about twenty minutes. Then fighter bombers will drop bombs and napalm on the area. Finally, the helicopter gunships of our own division would come in low strafing and firing rockets," I told them.

Just before sunrise and zero hour, the first sergeant informed me that one man refused to go. "Bring him in here," I ordered.

The kid was not more than nineteen. His eyes were like saucers, his speech uncertain, stammering. I tried to calm him down. I may have even put my arm around him. "Son, if you refuse to go, I'll have to put you up on charges. You'll go to Leavenworth for twenty-five years. Your life will be ruined. Beside, I've been on one hundred and eighty of these airborne assaults and I'm still here. I tell you what, you fly in my helicopter and I'll follow you through on all this. You'll be alright."

Reluctantly, he agreed to go. A hundred helicopters rushed in and took us to the landing zone, eighteen of them just for our company. Fffttt-ffftt-fffttt, engines whining, dust flying, orders being barked- it was pretty chaotic even for the veterans

Just before jump off, the helicopter hovers at about six feet and we jump. I was trying to read our altitude and leaned out the door. A grab bar at the side of the door kept me in but leaning drastically.

Machinegun bullets began striking the helicopter and tore the grab bar loose. I hit the ground with a thud. Standing up trying to catch my wind, I looked back at the chopper. The kid was lying flat on his back with both legs dangling out the door. His helmet was on the ground splattered with blood and brains. He had been hit twice in the head. I threw the helmet into the chopper and yelled, "Take him back."

Leavenworth didn't seem so bad after all. I didn't kill the poor kid but his memory still haunts me. Decisions of command- damn them. And somewhere in Kentucky, a family was asking, "How can that be? He just left a week ago."

180

When my promotion to major came through, I took R&R and went to Hong Kong. My replacement was a captain who had no combat experience, none at all.

The night before my return to the base, the company sector was attacked by a large North Viet Namese force. I was met at the tarmac by the company 1st sergeant, a Sgt. Ralph Canitz. He was frantic, on the verge of tears, "This wouldn't have happened if you were here. The new CO is dead and seventeen men with him. Sir, he didn't know what the fuck he was doing. The lieutenant is over there in the medical tent. They want to amputate his leg. He's been asking for you all morning. "

I hurried to the medical tent to find the anguished lieutenant. "They want to cut off my leg, Sir. Can't they take me to a hospital like Walter Reed or someplace and save it?"

"I'll ask the doctors. I'll be right back." I responded.

After conferring with three surgeons I came to a conclusion. He would take five days to get back to a hospital in the States and would either bleed to death or die from infection. I gave the lieutenant the bad news. For some reason he trusted me more than the doctors. He finally agreed, "I respect your opinion, Sir. Take my leg off." And fifty years later it bothers me. I like to think that somewhere in Middle America there is a 64 year old man with one leg and two armfuls of grandkids. I hope I made the right decision.

The 1st Sgt. Ralph Canitz was fighting in Viet Nam after being in the Korean War. He had a small round scar next to his nose where a bullet had struck him. Miraculously it found a safe route through his head and exited at the back of the skull. I believe his good fortune continued and he left Viet Nam safely.

When I left Viet Nam the second time I was even more convinced I was lucky to be alive. Besides the bullet through the arm, one had traveled through my bulky fatigue jacket, in one front pocket and out the other. The war had intensified by leaps and bounds, the enemy more formidable.

In 1971 I was asked to sign a disclaimer saying that if I was

181

captured by the enemy the US Government would deny that I was a member of the United States armed forces. This was a bit disconcerting to me since I had just completed a year long course for advanced pathfinders. The class of 27 was selected from 400 applicants. The mission I had volunteered for was TOP SECRET, involving cross border operations into Laos and Cambodia and even to North Viet Nam.

We wore black fatigues, carried weapons that were either sterile or of foreign manufacture. Nothing could tie us to the United States. Three different times I went into North Viet Nam, always at night, always with a great deal of apprehension.

The enemy's Ho Chi Minh Trail ran through parts of Laos and Cambodia and yet the media treated that lightly and thought our presence there would be "expanding the war." Other American units had been engaged there for years, secretly directed by the CIA. North Viet Nam and the Pathet Lao communists had been fighting there as well as moving supplies.

My new assignment was a staff position for I Corps CO, Lt. Gen.Welborn Dolvin, a sort of operations aide-de-camp. The country was divided up into Command and Control South, Central and North for purposes of launching attacks across the borders. After a few months I was given command of the Command and Control North.

In preparing for one operation across the border, I came to the conclusion that this was a bad idea. I expressed my concerns in person to Gen. Creighton Abrams. The operation was aimed at getting information on large armored columns coming down the main arteries towards Saigon. He wanted twenty-four observation teams sent north to monitor their movements. Knowing the dangers and the low probability of getting additional intelligence I suggested we try one team. He agreed.

The twelve men went in at night and immediately came

under heavy fire. Two men were wounded and a third already killed when we got the call for help. The team leader said he was in the middle of an entire division and under intense fire. We sent the choppers back to get them.

Each man had to be lifted on a rope suspension chair back to the chopper. In the dark and under fire the recovery guys did a great job except one man got his foot caught in the limbs and vines. When the helicopter pulled up, his foot was pulled off at the ankle.

The general finally agreed to call off the operation. We were told to stand down. For seven weeks we stood down and then we left Viet Nam. Before we did, Gen. Abrams was elevated to Chief of Staff of the Army and left for Washington. Two years later he was stricken with cancer and died in September of 1974. I never had occasion to speak again with the general, so I don't know if he called off the operation because he agreed with me, or if some other power intervened. Saigon fell seven months later.

Before the war had ended seventeen of my twenty-six classmates in the advance pathfinder course were dead or missing in action. Three were Medal of Honor recipients, all posthumously. It was a dangerous business and yet 400 men had applied to do it. You could say they were crazy. I like to think they were motivated. The foreign mercenaries were second or third class but the American GI was first class, many a cut above that. I saw them fight, I led them and I couldn't be more proud of them. Now after fifty some years I still get choked up thinking about them. The older I get, the more frequently that occurs. From the recesses of my aging mind, the 1st Cav trooper who lost his leg surfaces most often. I see his face so clearly, but his name escapes me.

**Capt. Jack Conlon enroute to Viet Nam
Pauses at WWII Guam battle site, 1964**

**Col. Jack Conlon with daughters
Colleen (R) and Cathleen (L)
at his retirement in June, 1981**

Jack Conlon loves life and lives it to the fullest. He took his chances like the rest of us though. Our families and our military training prepared us to face life's challenges.

- Roger H.C. Donlon (MOH),12/30/2010

Conlon battles for 1975 U.S Forces Karate title in Korea
where he finished 1st in heavyweight division

Conlon acted as guide for entertainer Martha Raye in '72
She prepares to drink her morning toddy.

There was a part of this war that isn't discussed very much. When a man was killed, his next of kin had to be notified by a Notification Officer. The next day, another officer would contact the family and inform them of their survivor benefits. As a professor of military science at Furman University, it was my duty to provide those services to next of kin located in western North Carolina. One or the other of the two duties fell upon me thirty-five or forty times.

The scenario was almost always the same. The mom would break down crying before I had said the first word. The dad would try to hug her and hold her on her feet. My duty was to explain what had happened without getting caught in the emotion of the situation. I had seen men die, seen them dismembered and some totally disappear in an explosion. I think I performed those duties as well as anyone could because I had been subjected to that grief so many times before. It never is easy.

The more I traveled those back roads to Wilkesboro and Waynesville and Bryson City, the more I realized that it was the common people who shouldered the heaviest load. Their sons got no college deferments; they accepted the call to duty when their lottery numbers came up low. They fought and too many of them died. By 1971 the administration was fighting a war they knew they could not win. The lack of resolve and the lack of leadership left our troops fighting without an aggressive attitude and in that defensive posture they were asked to fail.

The draft, the lottery, the restrictions were all unfair. We could not bomb Hanoi, or mine the harbor at Haiphong. We could not invade past the DMZ. We could not win-- that was the most unfair of all. And yet we sent our most common citizens to do the fighting and most of the dying; they had the least to gain. At eighteen or nineteen, they had the most to lose. "His remains will arrive in seven to ten days," and the anguish, the tears and the twisting guts would start anew.

The Legion of Merit

Combat Infantryman's Badge

THIRTY

SURPRISE EVENTS IN THE TONKIN GULF

Captain Robert Hall, USN retired, recalls some surprise events while flying for Squadron VA-35, the Black Panthers from the USS Enterprise. Often life threatening, at times career threatening, events are often unexpected even for a carrier pilot. A graduate of Iowa State University and commissioned through ROTC, this is his story.

Spring of 1968 had arrived in the Tonkin Gulf; the Tet Offensive was now history, and Hanoi and Hyphong were off limits for US military strikes. The USS Enterprise (CVAN-65) steamed around the Tonkin Gulf a few miles off the North Vietnam coast line, where it shared the bombing responsibilities with another aircraft carrier. Carrier Air Group Nine was aboard the Big "E" with its complement of A-4 and A-6 attack bombers, F-4 fighters, E-2B early warning aircraft, H-3 search and rescue helicopters, A-5 photo reconnaissance aircraft and A-3 intelligence gathering aircraft. Air operations aboard the USS Enterprise were being flown in typical cyclic operations with launches and recoveries scheduled every ninety minutes over a twelve hour period. Multi-aircraft high casualty "Alpha" strikes were a recent thing of the past and most missions now were flown with only one or two aircraft. The flying environment was definitely not as hostile, as far as we were concerned, but we were still losing an occasional aircraft and crew.

I was assigned to the A-6 Intruder squadron, VA-35, called the "Black Panthers", not to be confused with the extremist group based at the time in San Francisco. The A-6 aircraft was flown by two Navy or Marine Corps crewmen, one a pilot and the other a bombardier-navigator (B/N) who was in charge of the computer, navigation and weapons systems. I was a Navy pilot and loved the A-6 for its integrated computer, radar and navigation system which was unique in the military. The A-6 design came from the frustrations of the Korean War where aircraft were pretty much limited to fly in VFR (Visual Flight Rules) conditions and lacked precision weapons delivery systems.

The A-6 solved that problem and could fly in all weather conditions, both day and night. On many occasions Intruders were the only aircraft flying over North Vietnam because of bad weather. The Intruder also had two engines, which could come in handy if one were to fail.

The A-6 carried ordinance on two stations under each wing and another station under the belly. A normal load for shipboard operations was 13 one thousand pound bombs (more than three times the load of a WWII B-17) or 22 five hundred pound bombs. The Intruder thus could accurately put a sizable amount of ordinance on a target. In addition we didn't use or need external fuel tanks in combat. The ship was close enough to the coastline which led to a relative short flight. The fighters on the other hand usually needed additional fuel during the flight, so we always had an air-wing tanker (refitted A-3 or A-6) airborne to help out.

I'd like to share a couple of stories to indicate how the

unexpected could happen during routine operations, if you could call dropping bombs in wartime routine!

On one particular cloudy night in that spring of 1968, the war with North Vietnam got personal. My B/N and I were assigned a target near the city of Vinh. For this mission our 22 five-hundred -pound bombs, were fitted with specialized "snake-eye" fins, which allowed the weapons to be dropped at low altitude with the aircraft able to safely escape the bomb fragmentation pattern. The snake-eye technology fins were installed to simply to slow them down. One unique feature about the 500 pound snake eye bombs was that the aircraft would shake slightly when they were released due to the disturbance in the air stream by the fins.

Right after our launch from Enterprise my B/N was able to give me a good heading to reach our point for entering the North Vietnam airspace. We turned off our external lights, crossed the beach without incident and continued on our route toward our target. We were flying on instruments in the clouds and couldn't see a thing, but that was fine with us. If we couldn't see the ground then the bad guys couldn't see us. We didn't know if the SAM (surface to air missiles) sites were up that night or not. We did know that Vinh was defended by a great number of antiaircraft guns up to 85 mm in size, but we figured they wouldn't be firing at us "in the blind". My B/N soon was able to identify the target on radar a few miles away and directed me to the release point using the on-board computer. The computer's software contained ballistic information for all the weapons the A-6 could carry. We accelerated to 420 knots and flew in at 1500 feet above the ground toward the target. The range was decreasing rapidly when all of a sudden the dark clouds started glowing around us. At the release point we felt the expected shudder of the bombs being released from the aircraft. Once past the target I banked the aircraft sharply to the left to egress the hostile area and return to the ship.

But the aircraft did not feel right. It seemed sluggish. I asked my B/N to use his flashlight and see if the bomb racks were clean. They were not. While he could only see a few bombs from his position, we suspected we had most or our entire load remaining. This happened occasionally due to an electrical glitch somewhere in the system. All of a sudden we realized that we had flown through "flak", the term used for exploding antiaircraft fire! Now what do we do? The bombs couldn't be released and we couldn't land on the carrier with such a heavy load. The emergency procedure was to fly back over the sea, turn south and then proceed over a hundred miles to our military base at Da Nang, South Vietnam. It was ok to land an A-6 at Da Nang with a full load of bombs, as long as we were careful and landed with a minimal rate of descent. I thus requested permission to divert so the bombs could be safely off loaded, and then we could return to the ship. But the folks on the Enterprise had other plans. I was directed to fly back to the ship and climb to 10,000 feet, where another aircraft could look us over and determine our bomb load. So we flew the 50 to 60 nautical miles back to the ship and by the time we finally joined up with another aircraft I had used up quite a bit of fuel. We were told that we did indeed have all our bombs and were now instructed to divert. The only problem was I now did not have enough fuel to safely fly to Da Nang. So we had to rendezvous with the alert tanker which was flying at another altitude and off we went to find him. In-flight refueling usually is not a difficult task, but throw in the fact it was night and we HAD to have gas and my hand holding the flight control stick was kind of tense. If this didn't work, and the emergency bomb rack jettison failed as well, we would have to eject and the Navy would be out one expensive aircraft. But after a couple of attempts we were able to plug into the basket and took on enough fuel to get us to the divert field.

The rest of the flight that night was pretty uneventful. We landed safely at the Da Nang airfield and taxied to the US

Marine Corps A-6 outfit. The Marines were happy to receive 22 perfectly good 500 pound bombs. The electrical problem was not identified except for a tripped circuit breaker in the nose wheel well, which could not be reset from the cockpit. That's why the bombs had not released. After a couple of beers (a good swap for a bunch of bombs!), we slept in a sandbagged protected hut and returned to the ship the next morning like nothing had happened. That evening we were back on the schedule for another flight and probably said a little prayer that none of the circuit breakers would pop that night. Flying through flak, refueling at night and a couple of beers on the beach made for another routine flight in the Tonkin Gulf.

A few days later we were scheduled for a mission in beautiful weather conditions in which any of the Enterprise aircraft could fly. On that day the A-4 Skyhawks were in the air. The Skyhawk was a small single engine jet aircraft also used for bombing targets in North Vietnam., but carried a much smaller load than the Intruder. A few weeks earlier "high value" targets in or near Hanoi or Hyphong were placed in a no-fly zone and we now were sent to second rate targets, such as rebuilt road bypasses or "suspected" ammo dumps. Our target on that day was just a few miles from the beach in a weakly defended area of North Vietnam. The mission was anticipated to be short in duration with minimal time over hostile territory. It was going to be a piece of cake, very different from the intensely hostile environments we were flying just a few weeks ago farther north.

Our flight that day went without a hitch and we returned to the safe area overhead the Enterprise which operated not far from the coastline. We had about 30 minutes before our planned landing time and I decided to do what all young, fearless bomber pilots do with time on their hands, pretend to be a fighter pilot. In those days just about any bomber pilot would look for another unsuspecting aircraft to "jump" and engage in a pretend dog fight to see who was king of the mountain, so to speak. Keep in mind the A-6 and A-4 do not carry guns or air to air missiles and thus cannot carry out the air superiority role that the F-4 had to defend the fleet. But we could pretend, couldn't we?

And so it happened that an A-4 Skyhawk jumped me that day, or maybe it was the other way around. At any rate we were putting our aircraft through some pretty tight turns and loading up the "G" forces and it looked like a standoff, until I slowed the Intruder deliberately and lowered the flaps in order to increase lift and be able to generate a quicker rate of turn. Now putting down the flaps in the A-6 in a "dog fight" was probably forbidden, since the flaps were only designed to assist in landing the aircraft. But wow did that aircraft turn and pretty soon I had the upper hand of our fight. The A-4 pilot (whom I won't name) applied additional G-forces to try to evade my aircraft, and seemed to be "escaping" until...his single engine quit...flamed out is the term we use. The Skyhawk pilot valiantly attempted to relight (start) the engine using recommended procedures, but the aircraft would not start again. He ejected a few seconds later and the Skyhawk was lost at sea.

After landing my Intruder aboard the carrier and after the Skyhawk pilot was rescued by the Search and Rescue helicopter, we were both ordered to report to the Carrier Air Group Commander to explain our actions. We were guilty of mistreating government property. What could we say? Because of our actions, all unofficial dog fighting was forbidden and we caught a lot of grief from friends. The maintenance personnel in the A-6 squadron were so impressed that someone painted a miniature A-4 on the fuselage of the A-6 similar to other fighter aces in times past.

Fast forward to 1975 when I had the fortune of teaching at the United States Naval Academy, and spent time trying to improve my golf game. It was during one of my golf outings that I was playing with an older gentleman, who happened to

194

be a retired Vice-Admiral and the uncle of the unlucky A-4 pilot. I started to share the story with all the aeronautical details, when he quickly cut me off and said he was not amused and had chewed out his nephew royally, when he had first heard of the story. I quickly changed the subject, and said something like, "How did you cure your slice?", or something like that.

Fast forward again to 2006 when this same A-4 Skyhawk pilot and I met at a retired naval aviation activity and we were reminiscing about that fateful day. He shared that he knew the aircraft had known engine problems. He decided to fly the mission anyway and wound up putting the aircraft through a lot more stress than it was capable of handling.

The A-4 pilot that day in April, 1968 was a navy lieutenant, who would rise to the rank of navy captain and have the command of an aircraft carrier. I would also achieve the rank of captain and command a major shore establishment.

I guess that single incident in the Tonkin Gulf kept us both from achieving Flag Rank. Yeah right.

An Intruder prepares for steam catapult launching from the deck of the USS Enterprise.

195

Lt. Bob Hall displays his bomb load.

Lt. Bob Hall aboard the USS Enterprise receiving 1st Air Medal for 20 missions over North Viet Nam, Seventh Fleet Commander presenting.

An A-6 Intruder of Squadron VA-35, the Black Panthers

THIRTY-ONE

THE LONGEST DAY OF THE SHORTEST TOUR

Sgt. Dennis O'Hare, of Albany, New York, had been in-country one day after in-processing when he went on his first patrol. Stationed at Con Guioc, seven miles south of Saigon, with the 199ᵗʰ Light Infantry Brigade, his tour met a sudden and unexpected turn. This is his story.

T he normal tour "in-country" during the Vietnam War was one year. Mine was one day, not counting flight days and in-processing. I was a newly minted NCO, a "shake and bake," out of Fort Benning with a TDY stint at Fort Dix as an advanced infantry training sergeant. Not bad work for someone who was a high school teacher a year earlier but here I was, in country, the summer of 1969, and I'm ready.

Camp Frenzell Jones, just outside of Saigon, was home to the Redcatchers, the BMB of the 199th Light Infantry Brigade. It sounded like something right out of Tennyson except we used helicopters and our muddy boots to patrol and protect Saigon's southern flank from Victor Charlie. The 199th units had all been greatly decorated throughout their colorful regimental histories going back to the 1700's and the time of George Washington. One regiment was the "Old Guard" now still seen in its high place of honor in ceremonial duties at our nation's Capitol. My regiment was the 3rd of the 7th infantry, the Cottonbalers, so called for the battle of New Orleans where they, along with Colonel Jackson, Old Hickory, fought behind bales of cotton. They were ready.

I was assigned to Delta Company, 3rd of the 7th that was just coming off a brief stand down in Con Giuoc, south of Saigon, and, on my first day, was going back out on patrol, the new guy included, to check on recent VC activity in our area. "I'm ready" I quickly quipped to the guys. Assuring myself took a little longer. A short briefing and off we went. A short Huey ride and a long slog through knee deep muck brought us to recent VC sightings. A Loach (light observation helicopter) suddenly buzzed closely overhead. It was not much larger than a dragonfly, a large plastic bubble with two guys inside. The pilots waved at us to get our heads and butts down as they lobbed at least half dozen grenades out their door. They were hoping to spook Charlie (but not us?) and give us a read. Nothing spooked, so up and off we went again. *I'm ready*. We were tracking a mud trail through the bush when BANG, it went off. I had just stepped on a mine or some buried device. After the loud bang there was even a louder silence. The yells and moans came later, first from the guys in back and front of me and after stunned shock and disbelief, my own. "I'm still alive and conscious." The muck seemed to have turned this device into a shaped charge, meaning most of the force went straight up and past the outside of the heel of my boot. My calf, thigh, buttock and elbow however were a little too close to the "straight up" part. The rest of me as well as the other guys were all intact and alive.

THE LONGEST DAY OF THE SHORTEST TOUR

The overhead Loach with the hand grenades was not a medevac equipped helicopter, but the captain radioed it down to get me out of there and to a hospital- fast. A little morphine (a lot actually) and a quick field dressing wrap of my calf and I'm ready.

They folded me up like an accordion, no stretchers here, and stuffed me behind the copilot's seat in the bubble. One of the pilots turned and said "Hey Sarge, the bad news is you're going to need some serious medical help; the good news, you're going home." He explained how President Nixon recently ordered that if you were wounded enough to leave country you weren't going to be sent back. He patted down my pockets until he found my cigarettes, a K ration 4 pack of Marlboros. Taking one out, he lit it. After a deep drag he expelled a long cool exhale. I was too weak to object. Turning around to me, he placed the cigarette in my mouth. "We'll be there in a minute, Sarge."

Maybe it was more than a minute, but the cigarette was finished when we landed. They unfolded me from behind the seat and stretched me out on a gurney. It was Saigon Field Army Hospital where they rolled me across the tarmac, doing a triage/diagnosis en route. Flipping me over and cutting my boots, belts, and underwear; flipping me over again and I'm in my birthday suit and dripping blood. The gurney rolled across the tarmac; a nurse strategically placed a wash cloth on me. Chaplain, now keeping the pace; "You're a brave man, Sergeant; we'll do the praying if you do the hanging on." *I'm ready*, I thought.

I awoke a day later. They say I had been in an operating room for 45 minutes to an hour and that they wired me together in the leg, pulled all the big chunks out of my multiple fragmentation wound (MFW) and bandaged up and stabilized me. A well choreographed procedure proved that the medical staff was getting to practice it all too often. But that is someone else's story, I'm sure. They were telling me the extent of my injuries, the fact that I was hearing them at all was relatively good news, a blessing. The other Redcatchers were all back with their company and the 199th LIB to finish out their tours. I was soon headed for Camp Drake in Zama, Japan to *stabilize*, and then on to Valley Forge Army Hospital in Pennsylvania to *recuperate*. Valley Forge, where George Washington and his army spent their longest winter and where I finished up my shortest tour.

Just before I left Saigon a full bird colonel came on to the floor to present me with a medal. He knows there's not much "ten hut" going on in the ward and he graciously pinned it to my pillow, The Purple Heart, the one with the face of George Washington.

"Cottonbalers by God, Damned Good Soldiers"

Sgt. Dennis O'Hare, Stonehill College '66

They give Purple Hearts for a reason, because getting wounded is a traumatic experience. It happened to me more than forty years ago and yet it seems like yesterday. 997 American service men died on their first day in Viet Nam. In that regard, I guess I was lucky. I never saw the enemy and yet one of them almost killed me. Sometimes I wonder if he fared as well as I did. Did he age gracefully; get gray hair and a touch of arthritis? Or...

THIRTY-TWO

MEMORIES

W hen Congress voted to remove all funding for the war in 1972, a new policy was put into action to make the South Viet Namese take over the war. Doomed to failure, it was at first titled *De-Americanization*. Later, it was renamed *Vietnamization*. The new policy bought a new group of advisors to Viet Nam, communications experts, infantry advisers, logistics and supply officers. Since helicopters had become such an integral part of ground operations, South Vietnamese non-coms and officers would have to be trained to fly them. After a lengthy language school, they were put through the rigors of helicopter flight school. In all, this was a two year process and time was running out.

Security advisor Daniel Elsburg gave it little chance and went as far as to say, "I don't believe there is a *win* option in Viet Nam." A weak South Viet Namese government ensured its failure. Soviet Ambassador to the U.S., Anatoliy Dubrynin, meanwhile dabbled with Nixon's chief ambassador Henry Kissinger, but the war continued.

By the spring of 1972 - 400,000 American troops had been

withdrawn and Pres. Nixon was able to continue to negotiate with both the Soviets and Chi-coms. In the North, Ho Chi Minh saw this as an opportunity to launch a massive ground attack supported by tanks and artillery. To his dismay, American airpower was still in play and the Communist force was beaten badly in *Operation Linebacker*.

By 1973 the revised Army of South Viet Nam (ARVN) continued to have problems of control, communications and reconnaissance. The North Vietnamese left the negotiation table in Paris believing they held all the trump cards. Nixon played his last one, *Linebacker II (Dec18-29)*. American fighter bombers and B-52s pounded Hanoi with 20,000 tons of bombs. The SAMs were nearly depleted and their interceptor aircraft down to a few. The North Vietnamese returned to the table in Paris.

When the end came and Saigon fell, General Norman Schwarzkopf watched on TV and cried. 58,000 American families would never be the same, four Notre Dame families among them. Four others would lose their Notre Dame men to training accidents.

In June of 2009 the Notre Dame Class of 1959 dedicated a bronze plaque on the Notre Dame campus to those eight men. It is located on the second floor of the Pasquarella Center ROTC Building.

THE CLASS OF 1959 DOES SOLEMNLY ACKNOWLEDGE

THE ULTIMATE SACRIFICE OF OUR FALLEN CLASSMATES.

THEY HAVE HONORED GOD,

THEIR COUNTRY AND NOTRE DAME.

1st Lt RICHARD S. HORSFALL, USMC - 02 NOV 1962

2d Lt LEONARD J. LeROSE, USAF - 23 DEC 1963

Capt EDWIN G. SHANK JR., USAF - 24 MAR 1964

Lt JOHN G. BYRNE JR., USN - 1965

Capt JAMES J. CARROLL, USMC - 05 OCT 1966

Lt CURTIS R. BAKER, USN - 28 MAR 1967

Lt EUGENE M. VAICHULIS, USN - 30 SEPT 1968

Lt Col JAMES A. FOWLER, USAF - 06 JUNE 1972

**Alumni Executive Director Chuck Lennon '61 with
Joe Mulligan '59 and Maj. Stephen Fowler**

Father Edward 'Monk' Malloy, CSC blesses the plaque

Maj. Stephen Fowler, Greta Baker Allen,
Patricia Horsfall Wilson, her son Keith and daughter Jennifer

Dan Rapp, Greta Baker Allen and
Col. Ed Mezzapelle USAF Ret.

THE CLASS OF 1959 DOES SOLEMNLY ACKNOWLEDGE
THE ULTIMATE SACRIFICE OF OUR FALLEN
CLASSMATES.

THEY HAVE HONORED GOD,
THEIR COUNTRY AND NOTRE DAME.

1ST Lt RICHARD S. HORSFALL, USMC - 02 NOV 1962

2ND Lt LEONARD J. LeROSE, USAF - 23 DEC 1963

Capt EDWIN G. SHANK JR., USAF - 24 MAR 1964

Capt JOHN G. BYRNE JR., USMC - 02 MAR 1965

Capt JAMES J. CARROLL, USMC - 05 OCT 1966

Lt CURTIS R. BAKER USN, - 28 MAR 1967

Lt EUGENE M. VAICHULIS, USN - 30 SEPT 1968

Lt Col JAMES A. FOWLER, USAF - 06 JUNE 1972

June 5, 2009

Near the site of the ancient battle of Marathon in southern Greece stands a limestone monument with 192 names. Now 2500 years old, it is the only historical record of the Athenians who died there. Greek historian Herodotus would name only their leaders, Miltiades and Callimachus.

A mere forty years after Viet Nam our committee was unable to find the circumstances surrounding the deaths of some of our classmates. Even the Department of Defense could not help us and so we gaze at our bronze plaque hoping our fallen classmates, like the Athenians at Marathon, will never be forgotten.

The war, no matter how tragic, was an honorable undertaking. Our leaders, Presidents Kennedy and Johnson, decided to stop the spread of Communism in South East Asia.

The 58,000 Americans who died there, died in vain, not because they were defeated on the battle field, but because the will to win was eroded by negative forces at home.

These same defeatists then turned a blind eye to what followed. Two million Cambodians died in the Killing Fields of the Khmer Rouge and a half million in Laos to the Pahtet Lao. Another 100,000 Viet Namese died in indoctrination camps and escape attempts in rickety boats. The media meanwhile claimed the "Domino Theory" never happened. More than two and a half million victims were never embraced by the same people who thrive on victimhood.

History reports warfare in terms of killed and wounded, but often ignores the fact that those statistics are someone's son, someone's brother or someone's husband. The lethality of warfare is devastating to the very fabric of civilization, the family.

For this reason, we have made it our goal to remember our classmates at Notre Dame with the plaque cast with their names. And to the litany of *someone's*, we would like to add, someone's friend, someone's classmate.

- Daniel P Rapp '59

Classmates Lost in Training Accidents
(Photo of Capt. Eugene M. Vaichulis, USN not available)

2nd Lt. Leonard J. Le Rose, USAF

Capt. John G. Byrne, US

1st Lt. Richard S. Horsfall, USMC

"We had been told, on leaving our native soil, that we were going to defend the sacred rights conferred on us by so many of our citizens settled overseas, so many years of our presence, so many benefits brought by us to populations in need of our assistance and our civilization.

"We were able to verify that all this was true, and, because it was true, we did not hesitate to shed our quota of blood, to sacrifice our youth and our hopes. We regretted nothing, but whereas we over here are inspired by this frame of mind, I am told that in Rome factions and conspiracies are rife, that treachery flourishes, and that many people in their uncertainty and confusion lend a ready ear to the dire temptations of relinquishment and vilify our action.

"I cannot believe that all this is true and yet recent wars have shown how pernicious such a state of mind could be and to where it could lead.

"Make haste to reassure me, I beg you, and tell me that our fellow-citizens understand us, support us and protect us as we ourselves are protecting the glory of the Empire.

"If it should be otherwise, if we should have to leave our bleached bones on these desert sands in vain, then beware of the anger of the Legions!"

Marcus Flavinus,
Centurion in the 2nd Cohort of the Augusta Legion,
to his cousin Tertullus in Rome

Nothing has changed.

Made in the USA
Columbia, SC
28 June 2022